WINSTON CHURCHILL
THE GREAT MAN'S LIFE
IN ANECDOTES

WINSTON CHURCHILL

THE GREAT MAN'S LIFE IN ANECDOTES

PATRICK DELAFORCE

FONTHILL

Fonthill Media Limited
Fonthill Media LLC
www.fonthillmedia.com
office@fonthillmedia.com

First published in the United Kingdom 2012
First published in the United States of America 2013

British Library Cataloguing in Publication Data:
A catalogue record for this book is available from the British Library

ISBN 978-1-78155-074-8 (print)
ISBN 978-1-78155-205-6 (e-book)

Typeset in Sabon 9.5/13
Printed and bound in England

Connect with us
 facebook.com/fonthillmedia 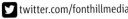 twitter.com/fonthillmedia

The Greatest Man of His Age

Winston Spencer Churchill (1874-1965) was one of the greatest Englishmen of all time, a true Renaissance man. Many of his skills and abilities are ignored by the history books, which concentrate on the fact that he was a soldier, politician, writer, orator and statesman. But he was also an inventor, novelist, pilot, cat lover, social reformer, gambler, bricklayer, racehorse owner, gardener, superb polo player, equestrian, painter of professional standard, *père de famille* ... and lover. Perhaps some of these attributes are part of an unfamiliar landscape to the reader of this book.

It is well known that he descended from General John Churchill, first Duke of Marlborough, who won the battles of Blenheim, Ramillies, Oudenarde and Malplaquet. And every biographical note will tell you that Churchill's father (the 'Music Hall Cad') was Lord Randolph, a talented, arrogant, difficult politician (and parent); that his mother was the beautiful American, Jennie, née Jerome, described by her son as 'The Evening Star'; and that Churchill's attractive, clever wife was Clementine, née Hozier, known to her husband as Mrs Grimalkin, Kat or Cat.

Churchill's initial fame came through his military and journalistic feats in the Boer War, which made him a national hero. As a young Hussar he craved the smell of cordite and the 'Baubles of Honour' when he came under fire in Cuba, the Malakand Pass, the Battle of Omdurman, Spion Kop, Antwerp, Ploegsteert; and later, during the London Blitz, Normandy, Naples and the river Rhine crossing. Secondly, as a politician, from the age of twenty-four and for the rest of his long life, he was a Member of Parliament, taking part in seventeen elections and by-elections, and also held a wide range of important ministerial posts. As Home Secretary he pushed through many vital social reform Bills, tackled strikes, witnessed first-hand the Battle of Sidney Street and tried hard to settle peacefully the tragic Irish situation. In 1911 he joined the Committee of Imperial Defence and wrote a memorandum predicting accurately the course of events in a future European War. As First Lord of the Admiralty he converted the Royal Navy from coal to oil power, increased the size of the battleship guns and accelerated the Navy's construction plans for new ships. He wrote detailed plans for the future army tank (HMS *Centipede*), the naval beach landing craft and the famous Normandy Mulberry harbours of 1944. Then came the role of Chancellor of the Duchy of Lancaster and, in 1917, he became Minister of Munitions, coordinating, with the British, French and American armies, a huge range of military and aviation equipment urgently needed for what was to be the last year and a half of the Great War. In 1919 he became Secretary of State for War and Minister for Air, responsible for the quick and efficient demobilization of three million servicemen — many on the brink of mutiny. Between the wars he was Colonial Secretary, dealing with the Irish and Middle East problems (including Iraq). From 1924 to 1931 he was Chancellor of the Exchequer, during which time Britain rejoined the Gold Standard (this turned out to be a mistake). In 1938 he was back at the Admiralty and from May 1940 to July 1945 was wartime Prime Minister, for which he became internationally famous. His close links with President Roosevelt were vital and he forged a rather dangerous alliance with 'Uncle Joe' Stalin, visiting him in the Kremlin and in Yalta. Thrown out of office in July 1945, as an MP he warned of the dangers to come of the 'Iron Curtain' as the Communists put a stranglehold on half of Europe. He painted and became a gentleman farmer at his beloved Chartwell Manor, laid bricks, organized the ponds, lakes, lawns, animals and house repairs. He became Prime Minister again from 1951 to 1955 and retired from Parliament in 1964, aged ninety. It is doubtful whether any British politician has had such a scintillating political record and one covering so many ministerial responsibilities.

His third major claim to fame was as a journalist and author. He wrote articles for most of the national papers, starting at the age of twenty-one. His first few books from 1898 concerned the coverage of 'his' wars in North-West India, Egypt and South Africa, and he wrote a novel, his only full-length work of fiction. He also wrote biographies of his father, Lord Randolph Churchill, and his ancestor, the first Duke of Marlborough, which were well received. His later works brought him fame and immense fortune, particularly the great history of the Second World War. In 1953 he was awarded the Nobel Prize for literature.

Churchill was also notorious for 'crossing the floor' in the House of Commons from Conservatives to Liberals, and then, amazingly, back again to the Tories. Churchill lived like an aristocratic pasha with a constant entourage of cronies (Max Beaverbrook, Brendan Bracken, 'The Prof' Lindemann and F. E. Smith, later Lord Birkenhead), as well as servants, secretaries, chauffeurs, security guards, nannies for his five children and 'visiting firemen' (politicians, journalists, generals and film stars). He and Clementine kept a good table, with Pol Roger champagne and Cuban cigars to fuel the 'Pasha's' creativity.

During their long married life, husband and wife exchanged 1,700 or more letters (edited and published by their daughter, Mary Soames). Churchill always dominated face-to-face discussions so Clementine put her sensible views to him in writing. Every letter gives a wonderful picture of a very happy and loving couple, with pet nicknames for themselves and for their children and friends. Often the signature is signed off with a small sketch of a cat or a dog. Clementine's advice was extremely shrewd on social, political and household matters, and she sometimes reproached her husband if he was being too harsh with his political staff. When Churchill was out of the country Clementine, at his request, cultivated appropriate cabinet ministers, generals and admirals (especially if his career appeared to be threatened), and she often lunched or dined with the Prime Minister of the day if her husband was abroad. She was

An Illingworth cartoon from the *Daily Mail* 27 July 1942. This was published three weeks before the disastrous Dieppe Raid of 19 August 1942.

a wonderful, deeply loving wife who put up with Churchill's impetuous and imperial manners and habits.

This book contains several hundred vignettes of all aspects of the couple's life, family, friends and enemies, and of Churchill's astonishing career, from Virginal Snowdrops to The Regency Rakes, from Lloyd George's Thumb to Boniface and the Golden Eggs, and many, many others.

Churchill with Lord Mountbatten at the Casablanca Conference, January 1943.

WINSTON CHURCHILL
The Great Man's Life in Anecdotes

The Music Hall Cad

Lord Randolph Churchill (1849-95) was the younger son of the seventh Duke of Marlborough, descended from General John Churchill, the celebrated victor of Blenheim, Ramillies, Oudenaarde and Malplaquet. Randolph became one of the more outrageous members of the royal entourage, enjoying high gambling, wild drinking and raffish house parties. He was amused by acrobats, jugglers and performing animals; he kept a string of race horses, and on the hunting field rode recklessly close to the hounds. A tireless traveller, he hunted lion in Africa, usually travelling with his valet and a lead-lined coffin — just in case. He entered Parliament in 1874, formed the 'Fourth Party', became Secretary of State for India, later Chancellor of the Exchequer and aspired to become Prime Minister. An ineffective debater whose insults and outrageous comments made him few friends, he was also an opportunist (which perhaps ran in the family). He was nicknamed the 'Music Hall Cad' and pictured by cartoonists as a dwarf with bulging eyes, flaring moustaches, a round head, wearing a loud suit, with his top hat at a rakish angle. He looked like an upper-class roué, which he was. His son Winston adored him — from a distance. Randolph was a true Victorian father — aloof, disdainful and mildly cruel to his offspring.

The 'Bankrupt New York Speculator'

Winston Churchill's mother, Jennie Jerome, was nineteen when she met Randolph at the Cowes Royal Regatta in August 1873. Their marriage took place in the

Jennie and Randolph photographed in Paris about the time of their marriage in 1874.

British Embassy Chapel in Paris on 15 April 1874. Her father, Leonard Jerome, came from an old Huguenot family and lived in New York, where he made and then squandered two fortunes on gambling, horse racing (he owned two race tracks) and opera singers. Randolph's father, the seventh Duke of Marlborough, described Jerome — the new in-law — as a 'bankrupt New York speculator'.

'The Evening Star'

To young Winston, his mother shone like 'the evening star', and although there was a great bond between them it was a somewhat distant relationship. Jennie was raven-haired with striking dark looks, a lively, high-spirited girl who grew up at the Imperial Court in Paris. She rode well, she was a good pianist, and enjoyed visiting exhibitions and museums. Her mother, who was reputed to have Iroquois blood, was nicknamed 'Sitting Bull'. Jennie was wildly extravagant and she and Randolph often ran into debt. They entertained royally (the Prince of Wales was a popular guest) at their various homes in Curzon Street, then Charles Street, and in Dublin. When Winston came of age she helped him greatly in advancing his military and journalistic careers.

More of the Panther

Edgar Vincent, 1st Viscount D'Abernon, wrote eloquently about the first time he saw Jennie, Churchill's mother:

'It was at the Vice-Regal Lodge at Dublin. She stood on one side to the left of the entrance. The Viceroy was on a dais at the farther end of the room surrounded by a brilliant staff, but eyes were not turned on him or on his consort, but on a dark, lithe figure, standing somewhat apart and appearing to be of another texture to those around her, radiant, translucent, intense. A diamond star in her hair, her favourite ornament — its lustre dimmed by the flashing glory of her eyes. More of the panther than of the woman in her look, but with a cultivated intelligence unknown to the jungle. Her courage not less great than that of her husband — fit mother for descendants of the great Duke.'

Jennie, Lady
Churchill
c. 1880.

'The Boy is Wonderfully Pretty'

In 1874 Gladstone and Disraeli bestrode the British political scene. Queen Victoria had been on the throne for thirty-seven years. The great British Navy guarded the trade routes, the sun never set on the British Empire and Pax Britannica, with some gunboat action and many dedicated young men running the colonies, brought relative peace to the world. Beer was a penny a pint. Fifty fresh eggs could be bought for a shilling. And on 30 November Winston Leonard Spencer-Churchill was born to Lady Randolph Churchill, née Jeanette (Jennie) Jerome, at Blenheim Palace, the Churchill family seat near Woodstock in Oxfordshire. Lord Randolph, the proud father, wrote to Jennie's mother, 'The boy is wonderfully pretty, so everyone says, dark eyes and hair, very healthy considering its prematureship.'

Jennie, Lady Churchill with young Winston c. 1876.

'Woomany': 'My Darling Winny'

Victorian parents were often very remote from their offspring, leaving them to the domestic staff and, later, boarding schools. Elizabeth Ann Everest, known to the Churchill family as 'Woom' or 'Woomany', was Winston's nanny. In early 1875, aged forty-two, she came from the Medway towns to become his surrogate parent and most intimate confidante. On discovering Winston's scars, received from the sadistic headmaster of his first boarding school, in Ascot, she persuaded Lady Randolph to remove him immediately. Later, when he went to Harrow school, it was she who visited him regularly. He rather bravely presented her to his friends as his 'Nurse'. Their correspondence reveals an affectionate and expressive relationship (he titled himself 'Winny' to her 'Woom') and this never faded. In later life she would write to her famous ex-charge: 'My poor sweet old precious lamb, how I am longing for a hug. Although you are not perfect, I do love you so much.' She died in 1895 and Winston and his brother Jack went to her funeral, paid for the headstone on her grave and were infinitely sad.

Left: Young Winston in a sailor suit.

Below: Elizabeth Anne Everest, the beloved nurse to Winston and Jack.

A Fairy Princess with a Diamond Star

Lord Randolph's father, the Duke of Marlborough, had been appointed by the Prime Minister to be Lord-Lieutenant of Ireland. Randolph was in disgrace. He had more or less blackmailed the Prince of Wales about an alleged romance with Lady Aylesford and boasted, 'I have the Crown of England in my pocket.' Queen Victoria was not amused. The young Churchills were blackballed by society and, early in 1877, took refuge with the Duke in Dublin, where Randolph became his private secretary. In *My Early Life* (1930) Churchill recalls a 'vision' of his mother as she hunted in Ireland; sat high on her horse, wearing a tight-fitting mud-spotted riding habit, regal and radiant like a fairy princess. She often wore a diamond star in her hair — her favourite ornament. It was in Dublin, in February 1880, when Winston was five, that his beloved younger brother John Strange Spencer-Churchill, known as Jack, was born.

'Menaced with Education'

Winston first suffered the trials of education at the Little Lodge near his grandfather's vice-regal residency. There, Mrs Everest produced a book, *Reading without Tears*, to encourage Winston's first faltering 'long path to erudition'. His nurse pointed with a pen at the different letters, but Winston was unimpressed with tuition, disinclined to learn and found the whole thing tiresome. A sinister figure described as 'the Governess' arrived in due course, and Winston took refuge in the Dublin woods, but he was retrieved and duly handed over.

'The Dismal Bog Called Sums'

Young Winston was in despair. Learning the alphabet and forming words was hard enough but the Governess was intent on teaching him elementary arithmetic. He had no time to play with his toys in the nursery (the thousand or so tin soldiers) nor to do interesting things in the garden. Great importance was now attached to the exact and accurate answer to 'the dismal bog called sums'. Jennie, of course, sided with the Governess. Life was certainly not fair.

Happy in His Nursery

Winston was sent to board, aged not yet eight, at St George's Preparatory School in Ascot, which was run by a tall, angular sadist with mutton-chop whiskers. The school was modelled on Eton, with ten boys to a class, a swimming pool and spacious games grounds, while the masters, all in gowns and mortar boards, were M.A.s. Winston was not too keen. For most of his childhood, until the age of seven, he had been surrounded by wonderful toys in his nursery, including a working steam engine, magic lanterns and toy soldiers. No surprise, then, that for young Winston the seven or eight hours of lessons to which he was now subjected at school were such a bore.

Matters were made worse by the fact that he was a somewhat troublesome child, and that, despite expecting to have many adventures and great fun living with other boys, he was frequently birched and hated the school.

A drawing of Winston
in his sailor suit
c. 1880.

Poetry, Riding and Swimming

St George's School, Ascot, marked Winston's progress as 'Geography and history, very good'; 'French and Classics, very fair to good.' And after a very slow start his spelling and writing were much improved. He recalled that in those days his greatest pleasure was reading. After Lady Randolph realized from the scars inflicted on him by beatings that he needed a different school, his education continued in a smaller, less pretentious establishment in Hove run by two spinsters, the Misses Kate and Charlotte Thomson. There, he found a place of education that gave him the freedom to learn those things that he was interested in, which included French, History, poetry, swimming and riding. In March 1886 the eleven-year-old collapsed at school with pneumonia. The family doctor, Robson Roose, sent daily reports to Lady Randolph. Winston recovered, played the piano in a school concert, acted in *The Mikado* and asked his mother if he could have cello lessons. Neither parent visited him, even though they went to Brighton on social occasions.

Winston aged about 10 at prep school.

Deputy Mother

Laura, Countess of Wilton, the daughter of William Russell and married to a rich landowner, a close friend of Winston's parents, befriended the young schoolboy. She sent him £2 a week pocket money from her house, The Hatch, near Windsor, and mandarins from her house on the French Riviera. Her letters started 'Dearest Winston' and ended 'With best love, Yr very affecte, deputy mother Laura Wilton.'

Books: *the Greatest Pleasure*

From the moment when his father gave him Robert Louis Stevenson's *Treasure Island*, Churchill was hooked on reading. Later, he remembered the pleasure with which he devoured *Treasure Island*, yet such prodigious reading puzzled his teachers, who saw at once a child reading more advanced books than his years would have suggested, and yet who still resided at the bottom of his form. He was nine and a half. He learned (just) the Greek alphabet but could not write a Latin verse. But he devoured Rider Haggard, reading *King Solomon's Mines* twelve times. He requested General Ulysses Grant's *History of the American Civil War* and favoured authors who wrote of high adventure:

Jack and Winston with their mother, *c.* 1888.

Winston at Harrow.

Rudyard Kipling, Robert Louis Stevenson, C. S. Forester's sea dramas, Sir Walter Scott. Later he much admired Charlotte Bronte, Guy de Maupassant, Somerset Maugham and Henry Fielding's *Tom Jones*. Much much later came Trollope's *The Duke's Children* and George Orwell's *1984*. He could recite from memory large chunks of Longfellow, Milton, Macaulay and Byron, as well as Edward Lear's books of nonsense rhymes.

'The Ordinary British Sentence': Harrow School

Lord Randolph consulted friends and Harrow public school was duly chosen. The headmaster, the Rev. J. E. C. Welldon, accepted Winston (despite his ignominious Latin prose exam — if Churchill's own account of it is taken at face value, the paper he handed in had little more than his name on it, a blot and several smudges) and on 17 April 1888, aged thirteen, he entered the Small House, run by Mr H. O. D. Davidson. The only subject he really enjoyed was English, which taught him from a young age about the structure of the noble 'British' sentence, a skill that would serve him so well in the years to follow. The assistant master sent a letter to Churchill's mother: 'His forgetfulness, carelessness, unpunctuality and irregularity in every way have really been so serious that I write to ask you ... to speak very gravely to him on the subject.' Nothing changed him. He joined the Harrow Rifle Corps, won the Public Schools fencing competition at Ascot, swam for his house in the school competitions, kept dogs secretly in a West Street house, gained a school prize by reciting 1,200 lines of Macaulay's *Lays of Ancient Rome* and could quote entire scenes from Shakespeare. He was always broke and needing extra pocket-money.

A Duelling Ground

During the school holidays from Harrow, Winston met at Lord Randolph's house many of the most pre-eminent members of the Parliamentary circle of the day. Such occasions bore witness to cordial political discussion between senior ministerial figures, including Arthur Chamberlain, Edward Carson, Arthur Balfour, H. H. Asquith and Lord Rosebery; impressive company indeed. Churchill was excited and inspired by these gatherings and the exchange of views that they provoked, and the great world of high politics impressed him greatly. However, while he observed that the business conducted between the men was often highly contested and the atmosphere was unforgiving, the meetings were, ultimately, pervaded by a sense of courtesy and respect, qualities that no doubt left their mark on young Winston. He later compared these occasions to the duelling ground.

Harrow School *c.* 1890.

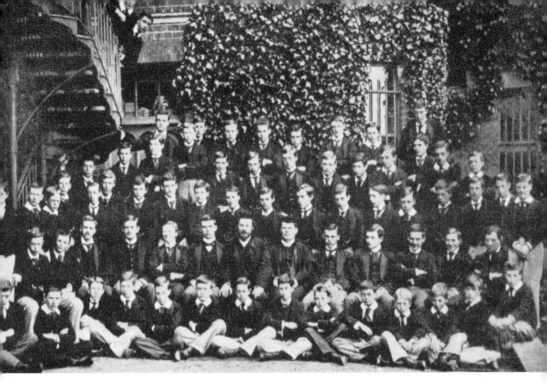

Winston Churchill at Harrow, 1892. This photograph was taken in Winston's second year at Harrow. He is the boy at the top of the fire escape steps.

A Loyal Partisan

In the autumn of 1892 Lord Randolph spoke to his teenage son at their house in Newmarket — one of only a handful of such conversations that Churchill could recall taking place between father and son. Lord Randolph's typical reticence vanished, and, to Winston, who was shortly to embark on a career in the army, he spoke and advised in an eloquent and mesmerizing fashion. At the end of their discussion, however, Churchill records how Lord Randolph made a plea to his son for latitude towards his misunderstood and misreported father, whose actions had often attracted controversy and complaint. Such public derision left no mark on Winston, however, who always remained a partisan to his father's cause, and a loyal son to an often difficult father.

A family group at Cowes *c.* 1892. Winston is seated to the right and his mother is seated on the arm of the chair. To her right is Winston's younger brother, Jack.

Soldiering on Horseback

After the three years in the Army Class at Harrow, Winston was sent to a crammer, the Captain James establishment in the Cromwell Road, London, in order to enter the Royal Military College at Sandhurst. It took three exam attempts and he eventually succeeded in 1893 — 95th out of 389 candidates. He missed the Infantry entry by 18 marks. That meant the cavalry, which would cost Lord Randolph (who was furious) an extra allowance of £200 to pay for chargers and horse-furniture. Winston was thrilled at the thought of soldiering on horseback, and believed it would be great fun owning a horse. Also, the cavalry uniforms were far more magnificent than those of the Foot (and more expensive). Lord Randolph made his son an allowance of £10 per month and paid his tailor and haberdasher bills. Duchess Fanny, his grandmother, also made him an allowance of £20 per month. Eventually Winston owned two official chargers, several hunters, as well as an indispensable string of polo ponies.

'The Awkward Squad'

As a Gentleman Cadet Winston Churchill studied Tactics, Military Administration, Drill, Gymnastics and Riding. He did not like the drill at Sandhurst and was seen as one of 'The Awkward Squad', having little talent for drill and for several months needing remedial instructions. Horses, on the other hand, were one of Churchill's greatest pleasures during his time at Sandhurst. He and his friends would often hire horses from local stables and gallop about the countryside, and organize point-to-point and steeplechase races on the estates of local landowners.

Although at Sandhurst the discipline was strict and the demands of academic study still plagued him, Churchill became deeply interested in Tactics and Fortification. His father encouraged him to acquire a number of works on military science, tactics and strategy, which included Hamley's *Operation of War*, Maine's *Infantry Fire Tactics* and various histories of a number of wars, including those of the Franco-German and American Civil wars.

Dyslexia?

Churchill's very disappointing academic record – undistinguished at Harrow, needing three attempts to gain entrance to the Royal Military Academy, Sandhurst, should be compared to, in his later life, great intellectual successes, including the Nobel Prize for Literature. This does suggest that he was possibly dyslexic?

Winston Churchill entered Sandhurst in 1893 as a cavalry cadet. He found his army training more enjoyable than his schooldays.

'Aladdin's Cave'

Winston Churchill was aged nineteen in 1893 and he urgently wanted a war — any war. In *My Early Life*, he wrote unequivocally about his youthful fervour for battlefield action, and recalled how, to him, the world seemed increasingly peaceful and harmonious, and that the end of the great days had come. Nevertheless, he reasoned, there were still a few isolated parts of the world where savage and wild peoples lived — peoples such as the Afghans and the Dervishes of Sudan — who could, he believed, be relied upon perhaps to provide some military distraction; even India could revolt. He would not have to wait for too long to find his war.

In December 1894 Winston passed out eighth of his batch of 150 cadets into this world, which like Aladdin's cave, opened before him. His father, who had, not long before, castigated him for his 'slovenly happy-go-lucky harum-scarum style of work', lived just long enough to witness his triumph. Lord Randolph died on 24 January 1895.

'Raise the tattered flag'

When his father died, aged only 46, Winston was devastated. All his dreams of comradeship with Randolph, of entering Parliament at his side and in his support, were ended. He determined to enter politics to vindicate his father's reputation and to 'raise the tattered flag from the stricken battlefield', which Lord Randolph had let fall.

The Young Popinjay with the 4th Hussars

Winston Churchill was commissioned on 20 February 1895 into the 4th Hussars, a well-known cavalry regiment, which had won a Victoria Cross in the famous charge of the Light Brigade in the Crimean War, while other battle honours included Talavera, Salamanca, the Alma and Balaklava.

Second Lieutenant Churchill looked a dashing young popinjay in the Hussar uniform — the dark blue tight tunic and 'overalls' (trousers), the elaborate gold frogging, the lace-entwined cuffs and collar and the striped trousers. Gold lanyards crossed his chest and a gold bandolier with a dispatch case was worn from his left shoulder. Patent-leather knee-high boots, swan-necked spurs and a black sealskin busby hat completed his martial attire. It took him six years to pay for these essential accessories.

The military year consisted of seven months' summer training and five months' winter leave. In the autumn of 1895 the 4th Hussars moved to

Winston Churchill was commissioned into the Fourth Hussars. He found his time as a recruit-officer which lasted six months most arduous, but at the same time much to his liking. In the same year he went to Cuba to gain experience of war at first hand.

Hampton Court and Hounslow, and Churchill, who lived at home with his widowed mother, travelled to Hounslow Barracks on the Underground.

He was involved in several minor scandals and gave himself over to the coruscating entertainments that London could provide to a moneyed member of an aristocratic family. He also enjoyed playing polo at Hurlingham and Ranelagh, and demonstrated early evidence of his skill at the sport that he would come to hold in such high regard. Churchill would become a crack polo player.

Cordite, Rum, Cigars and Siestas

Fortune smiled on the young Hussar at the end of 1895. He found a war, and he found a second and important career — in journalism. He and his friend Reginald Barnes obtained leave to observe a military campaign in far-distant Cuba, where Marshal Martinez Campos, commanding the Spanish occupation army, was endeavouring to catch and destroy elusive rebel forces. Sailing to New York and thence to Havana, Churchill and Barnes were attached to a Spanish column near the fever-ridden town of Sanctus Spiritus. When in the dim light of early morning Churchill first saw the shores of Cuba rise and define themselves from dark blue horizons he felt as if he sailed with Long John Silver and gazed on Treasure Island for the first time. This was a place where real things were going on, here was a place he might leave his bones. For a few weeks they meandered through tropical forests having occasional skirmishes. On occasion they came under fire when the rebels made a stand and then vanished despite General Valdez's efforts to capture them. The Cuban campaign, the 'Pearl of the Caribbean', he called it, produced the smell of cordite; he heard shots fired in anger, investigated rum cocktails and learnt the benefits of a Spanish siesta. Above all, he smoked Havana cigars — and did so for the rest of his life. General Valdez presented him afterwards with the Spanish Order of Military Merit, an enamelled cross with a white and red ribbon — a twenty-first birthday present, as it arrived on his birthday.

Writing for Money

Churchill asked his mother to act, unofficially, as his literary agent. He was forced to be discreet since the Armed Services did not approve of commercial undertakings by serving officers. With his correspondence to his mother he would often enclose letters or articles that he intended for publication in British newspapers or magazines; in one such missive to his mother, in September 1895, Churchill expressed the point that while he didn't know what terms she'd agreed with *The Daily Telegraph*, on no account should it be less than £10 per letter. Of course, he also recognized that maintaining a presence in the public eye through the media would perhaps prove useful in his later moves towards politics. Yet his journalistic transactions did not always go smoothly; on one occasion he considered himself 'defrauded' by an offer made by *The Daily Chronicle* of £10 per letter to cover events in Crete, and by way of historical support quoted Dr Johnson's famous maxim, 'no one but a blockhead ever wrote except for money'.

The *Daily Graphic* paid him five guineas (£5 5s., a generous fee in those days) for each of five articles entitled 'The Insurrection in Cuba'.

Bangalore: Garden of India

After his Cuban adventure Churchill made ready for the 4th Hussars' planned Indian Frontier expedition. He already had a sensible relationship with Colonel John Brabazon, his commanding officer, an Irishman who had devoted much of his life to the British Army. But in 1896 at Deepdene, near Dorking, home of his much-married aunt Lilian, he met Sir Bindon Blood, a very experienced

In 1897, Lieutenant Churchill went to India. Later he was attached to the 31st Punjab Infantry and was with the Malakand Field Force where he was mentioned in despatches and obtained a medal with clasp. He was later on the staff of Sir William Lockhart.

Indian Frontier general. Churchill was quick to extract from him a promise that if he ever commanded another expedition, Blood would send for him.

The 4th Hussars were destined for Bangalore, 2,000 miles from the NW Frontier and a centre for colonial rule. Churchill arrived in Bombay aboard the SS *Britannia* in October 1896. He promptly had an accident and dislocated his right shoulder, an injury that would haunt him throughout his life. A bad start indeed. On arrival, Churchill, Reginald Barnes (his fellow officer in Cuba) and Hugo Baring shared a palatial bungalow, its verandas bejewelled with flowers and creepers, and the air filled with butterflies — not for nothing was Bangalore known as the 'garden of India'. Churchill now had only two interests — polo and education.

'The Spanish Ships'

Churchill had, for much of his life, a slight speech defect which made him pronounce the letter 's' in a strange lisping hiss. He consulted a throat specialist who found no organic problem, so gave him speech exercises. Before Churchill left for India in 1896, his friends could hear him declaiming loudly, 'The Spanish ships I cannot see for they are not in sight.' He wrote to his mother aboard ship after a successful twenty-minute extemporary speech in a mock trial, reassuring her (and no doubt feeling reassured) that his vocal impediment didn't in any way affect his articulation.

Walden

Thomas Walden was the devoted butler and valet in the Randolph and Jennie household (wherever they went, even big-game shooting in Africa, he went too). Churchill's clothes were — before Sandhurst — ragged and unkempt and Walden did his best to keep the young boy reasonably smart. He was equal to every social occasion, even climbing trees on African lion hunts. When Lord Randolph died in 1895, he continued to valet Churchill and accompanied him in 1899 to South Africa.

India: Polo Chukkas in Bangalore

Churchill's pay in the Indian Army was 14 shillings a day plus £3 a month on which to keep two horses. His allowance from his mother, Lady Randolph, was £500 a year paid quarterly. If he was short of money he borrowed from the local native bankers, whom he found a pleasure in manner and intent, if somewhat avaricious. On board ship on the voyage out to India a regimental polo club was formed. Normally it would take two years after coming from England to make an impression on the highly competitive Indian polo teams; as well as all the cavalry regiments, all the Indian nizams, nawabs and princes, and Indian regiments fielded good teams. But on disembarkation the bold 4th Hussars purchased the entire polo stud of twenty-five Arabian polo-trained ponies from the Poona Light Horse, a native Indian regiment officered by the British. The Hussars played not just two or three times a week but every day, or rather every early evening. Despite his injured shoulder, Churchill played between eight and twelve chukkas — daily!

As a member of the regimental team they had high hopes of winning the All-India Inter-Regimental Tournament. They expected such a victory to come after several years of hard training and competition, but within six weeks of landing in India in October 1896, the 4th Hussars won the Golconda Cup, played in Hyderabad. On the first day they beat the famous Golconda team 9 goals to 3 and went on to win the tournament.

India: Bangalore and Education

Aged twenty-two, Churchill decided to improve his mind by intensive study, by reading history, philosophy and economics. He asked his mother's advice and every monthly mail-boat brought a package of books courtesy of Lady Jennie (who, incidentally, as a dashing widow, was having a marvellous time; Count

The lives of the officers revolved principally around their military duties — and polo, which was played avidly both for recreation and in a quest for the coveted Inter-Regimental Cup held by the best British team in India. Despite a shoulder injury, Churchill qualified to become a member of the regimental team and played the demanding sport skilfully. Polo was a near obsession for Churchill and the other polo-playing officers of the 4th Hussars: 'the serious purpose of life,' as he once described it. The highlight of the day was polo.

Charles Rudolph Kinsky, an Austrian diplomat on service in London was an ardent suitor.) Lord Randolph had read Gibbon's *Decline and Fall of the Roman Empire*, so his son now read the eight volumes during the long hours of the Indian afternoon. Next came Gibbon's *Autobiography* and Macaulay's *Lays of Ancient Rome*. From November to May he would read for four or five hours every day, history and philosophy: Plato's *Republic* and the Politics of Aristotle; Adam Smith's *Wealth of Nations*; Malthus on 'Population'; Darwin's *On The Origin of Species*. To gain some knowledge of recent British politics, Lady Randolph sent him the copies since 1870 of the *Annual Register*, a yearly review of Government business. Curiously, he asked for and studied intently Bartlett's *Familiar Quotations*, which probably came in useful later on.

Pamela Plowden: First Love?

In Secunderabad Churchill met a girl of dazzling beauty, the daughter of the British Resident in the dominions of the Nizam of Hyderabad. He rode with

Pamela Plowden on an elephant through the streets, dined with her parents and fancied himself in love with her. Shortly before returning to India he wrote to her in November 1898. Despite protestations of love there was no hint of passion. It was obvious that he had no intention of committing himself. In a desultory way they met and corresponded even after her marriage in 1902 to the second Earl of Lytton. They remained firm friends to the end of his life. She once said, 'The first time you meet Winston you see all his faults, and the rest of your life you spend in discovering his virtues.'

Affairs of State or Savrola

Churchill's only novel was written, 70,000 words of it, in dribs and drabs in Bangalore during 1897 and was finished by 20 May 1898. Its original title was *Affairs of State* and it was published in *Macmillan's Magazine* in 1900. Churchill confessed to his mother that the hero of the story was a mouthpiece for Churchill's own philosophies. The novel's purpose was to amuse and be full of wild adventure and atheistic philosophy. The highly dramatic romance took place in unhappy 'Laurania'. The key characters were President Antonio Molara, his wife Lucille, who was the most beautiful woman in Europe, and Savrola, who, of course, was the author himself, thinly disguised (Whig beliefs, ambition, polo-loving, catnapper, fits of depression and, naturally, brave and reckless under fire). There was also a devoted nurse. Inevitably Lucille and Savrola fell in love, but luckily Molara met his fate: shot by a terrorist! The book was dedicated to the officers of the 4th Hussars. *Savrola* was published also in the USA and earned Churchill £700, yet Churchill would say later in his life that he often dissuaded friends from reading it. A new edition was published in 1990.

Family Money Problems

In May 1897, with the approach of the hot weather season in Bangalore, Churchill took three months' accumulated leave. He sailed from Bombay in sweltering heat, rough weather and fearful seasickness, via the Indian Ocean and Port Said. He spent a fortnight in Italy seeing Rome and Pompeii and climbing Mount Vesuvius in the footsteps of Gibbon. Soon after his arrival in England he was in disgrace with his mother. A cheque of his for £50 had bounced at Cox's Bank; Jennie was horrified, adamant that if he could not live on his allowance he would have to quit the Hussars.

Lady Randolph and her elder son had expensive tastes. She received from Lord Randolph's estate £2,700 a year (approximately £150,000 at current values). After providing £800 in allowances for Winston and Jack, she paid £410 for house and stables rent. The balance of £1,500 had to cover servants, food, taxes and especially travelling and dress. The Hôtel Metropole in Monte Carlo was a favourite — so perhaps gambling was included in her annual budget.

The Seat of War

Young Churchill urgently wanted another war. Cordite of course, a medal or two, and to earn some money as a war correspondent. On the lawns of Goodwood Races he read in a newspaper that Sir Bindon Blood was leading a Field Force of three brigades to quell a revolt of Pathan tribesmen on the Indian Frontier. Churchill and his mother put out a 'three-line whip' to their family and friends. He sent a telegraph to Blood and took the train from London to Brindisi, then travelled by the Indian Mail Steamer to Bombay. He was giving up two weeks' leave for another possible military adventure. On his arrival he was greeted by General Blood's message: 'Very difficult: no vacancies: come up as a correspondent: will try and fit you in. B. B.' The Commanding Officer of the 4th Hussars was indulgent: 'Go and try your luck.' It took Churchill five days and nights by rail (and tonga pony cart) to travel the 2,028 miles to Nowshera, BB's HQ. When he had left London his friends said, 'He goes to the East tonight — to the seat of war.' Partly through his mother, two writing commissions were secured — the *Allahabad Pioneer* and the London *Daily Telegraph* at £5 per column.

Butcher and Bolt on the North-West Frontier

For centuries the North-West Frontier of India had been a battleground. Between 1858 and 1897 the British/Indian Army had sent thirty-four punitive expeditions against the tribesmen of the Swat valley bordering Afghanistan. Churchill described the Pathans as a somewhat barbarous people, with a vengeful nature and cruel customs. The region was guarded by British garrisons in a network of blockhouses and forts. The Pathan tactics were described as a butcher and bolt policy. One alternative was to offer the tribesmen 'subsidies' (i.e. bribes) to encourage good behaviour in that fearsome bandit country. Around this time Churchill wrote to his brother Jack and described how the damage inflicted by the tribesmen on the British forces and government must not simply be avenged; the 'Pax Britannica' must be maintained.

High Stakes in the Malakand Pass Campaign

Sir Bindon Blood, the force commander, wrote in his memoirs: 'My young friend Winston Churchill joined me as an extra ADC — and a right good one he was! ... I sent him over to join General Jeffreys in order to see a little fighting. He was all for it. He saw more fighting than I expected and very hard fighting too. He did excellent service with a party of Sikhs to which he carried an order, using a rifle borrowed from a severely wounded man.' Churchill was then attached to the 31st Punjabis and in a letter to his mother recounted how he waited until the very last moment before leaving the battlefront, despite the danger of his imminent death. He fired his revolver and forty rounds from the rifle, and thought that he'd hit at least four men. He undoubtedly acted bravely and also rashly, charging on his grey pony up and down the line while the other men took cover. He was honest about his motives for such an action: by his own admission he was a high-stake player; indeed, a captive audience inspired him to daring and noble acts. Following his successes in these engagements, Churchill felt confident that Sir Bindon would award him perhaps a medal and some clasps; he had already been made an orderly officer.

Tirah Field Force: Friends in High Places

Another North-West Frontier revolt broke out in September 1897 and General Sir William Lockhart's Field Force was sent to deal with the Afridi tribe in Tirah. Churchill was busy playing polo and writing, but he was determined to join in the fray. Overstaying his leave, he hurried to the railroad HQ at Peshawar, and having persuaded the General to appoint him as an extra orderly officer, he spent several weeks riding along the Frontier. The fighting petered out in March and April 1898. Churchill told his mother that he'd made the acquaintance of all the future generals; no doubt an important achievement for the ambitious man.

The Story of the Malakand Field Force

Churchill returned to Bangalore in mid-October 1897 and using largely the dispatches about the campaign which he had written (and been paid for) by *The Daily Telegraph* and *Allahabad Pioneer*, spent five weeks completing his first serious book — 300 pages and 80,000 words, which he dedicated to Sir Bindon Blood — and sent it off to Lady Randolph, who, via an agent, persuaded Longman to publish it in September 1898. The Prince of Wales sent Churchill an admiring letter but the reviewers castigated the appalling proofreading, which, in Churchill's absence, his mother had entrusted to her brother-in-law, Moreton Frewen, described in one review as a 'mad printer's reader'. From this book Churchill earned £700 (£30,000 in modern money) which helped pay for his quite expensive lifestyle.

Financial Difficulties

During 1897-8 Lady Randolph's financial affairs were so disastrous that she needed to take out a loan of £17,000 (almost a million pounds today) to pay her debts. The security was to be a life insurance policy on her life *and* on Winston's. She also arranged that he would guarantee the annual policy premium of £700 a year! Indignantly, he wrote to her on 28 January 1898, and made it quite clear that both he and she were excessively extravagant and cavalier when it came to money — and that, unchecked, such profligacy and self-indulgence would soon be their family's undoing. Churchill likened her buying a ball dress for £200 to his buying a new polo pony for £100. Since Lord Randolph's death three years earlier she had spent a quarter of the family's fortune.

Politics: Meeting 'The Skipper'

Churchill was determined to commence a political career and asked Lady Randolph to alert him if a political vacancy occurred as he wished to stand for election to the House of Commons. He forecast confidently that they would almost certainly elect him. He made three political speeches at Rotherhithe, Dover and Southsea, after an initial twenty-minute talk in July 1897 at a Primrose League fête near Bath, speaking in favour of the Workman's Compensation Bill. He made sure that a reporter from the *Morning Post* in a grey frock coat attended and that a whole column about him and his speech appeared the next day.

Early in November he paid a visit to the central offices of the Conservative Party at St Stephen's Chambers to enquire about finding a constituency. Mr R. W. E. Middleton, the Party Manager, known as 'The Skipper', was cordial and complimentary to Churchill, and expressed the Conservatives' agreement to garner for him a party seat, which would lead, all being well, to a place in Parliament in the near future. However, Middleton made it clear that a financial contribution to the constituency was essential, which quite dampened Churchill's hopes.

The Superior Oxford Prigs

In 1897 Churchill's support of the Tory party was ambivalent. In a letter to his mother he said that there were two among the leaders of the Tory party whom he despised and detested above all politicians: Mr Balfour and George Curzon. The one a languid, lazy, lackadaisical cynic, the unmonumental figurehead of the Conservative Party, the other the spoiled darling of politics — blown with conceit, insolent from undeserved success, the typification of the superior Oxford prig. He wrote that all the criminal muddles of the previous 15 months should be ascribed to the pair of them, and to 'Lord Salisbury, an able and obstinate man, who joins the brain of a statesman to the delicate susceptibilities of a mule'.

Glory in Egypt

There had been bloody revolts in the Sudan since 1882 and the Mahdi, a Muslim fanatic, defeated the British and Egyptian forces sent against him. General Gordon defended Khartoum, which fell, and he was killed in 1885. The Khalifa succeeded the Mahdi and created a huge army of Dervishes. Lord Kitchener was appointed Sardar as Commander of the Egyptian Army and in the spring of 1898 led a British-Egyptian army to avenge Gordon and recapture Khartoum. Churchill was now desperate to join Kitchener's Army. His mother's high-level influence failed completely. Lord Kitchener did not want this bumptious, well-connected young officer, who also appeared to be a journalist, on his staff. Churchill was very lucky. The Prime Minister, Lord Salisbury, had read and approved of the Malakand Campaign book and invited the author to 10 Downing Street. After the meeting, Churchill wrote to the Prime Minister suggesting he should telegraph to Lord Cromer, the political master of Egypt, recommending him and asking Cromer to inform Kitchener. Wheels within wheels? Two days later the War Office informed Churchill that he had been appointed a supernumerary lieutenant in the 21st Lancers for the Sudan Campaign. He then set sail to seek glory in Egypt.

Omdurman: the River Battle

Oliver Borthwick of the London *Morning Post*, by now a good friend of Churchill's, commissioned a series of letters about the Kitchener expedition into the heart of Africa at £15 per column. Travelling via Marseilles, Cairo, then joining the 21st Lancers, two weeks by train, stern-wheeled steamers,

Lieutenant Winston S. Churchill
attached to the 21st Lancers.

on foot, leading horses around the river Nile cataracts to Wadi Halfa, and, finally 400 miles across the desert, eventually took Churchill and the Lancers, as the cavalry advance guard, to within sight of the Dervish stronghold of Omdurman. On 1 September Churchill was the first man to sight the Khalifa's army and went off post-haste to report to Kitchener. The next morning twenty thousand British troops met the fanatical Dervish army, three times their size. The joys of Paradise awaited any who fell to Kitchener's artillery, Maxim guns and infantry rifle fire. As the Dervishes retreated, the 21st Lancers were ordered to charge and in doing so suffered 71 casualties, while 119 horses were destroyed. They won three Victoria Crosses on the day. Churchill claimed to have shot three men with his Mauser pistol, during the most dangerous few minutes of his life. A week later he started for home. The *Morning Post* paid him £300. He decided to leave the Army and write *The River War*. This book was published in November 1899 (and a cheaper popular edition in 1902). Churchill earned £4,000 for his Sudan adventure. However, his criticism of Lord Kitchener's needless desecration of the Mahdi's tomb and ill-treatment of the Dervish wounded after the battle didn't win him any favours with his superiors.

Five Objectives for 1899

Churchill planned for this year very carefully. He would return to India, play polo with the 4th Hussars and this time win the Polo Tournament. He would send in his papers and leave the Army. His finances might then relieve Lady Randolph from paying him the £500 annual allowance. He would complete writing *The River War* and obtain commissions from the *Allahabad Pioneer*. He would endeavour to enter Parliament. And this is, more or less, what he achieved.

India Again: the Prince of Games

In December 1898 Churchill sailed for Bombay, working on board ship, writing *The River War* and making friends with the eminent journalist C. W. Steevens of *The Daily Mail*, a fellow passenger. Churchill's objective was to help the 4th Hussars win the inter-regimental polo tournament at Meerut. On the way, at Jodhpur, their team was coached to improve their technique. Churchill had been playing No. 1 of a team of four when he had another accident, slipping and dislocating his right shoulder. Reginald Hoare, the captain, who played at No. 3, Reginald Barnes and Arnold Savory decided that the crippled Churchill should play with his arm strapped up because of his team-play knowledge and his experience of the game. It was a fairy tale as the 4th Hussars played the 4th Dragoon Guards in the final. The score was 1-2 and Churchill scored, 2-2; Churchill scored again, 3-2; then 3-3, and, unbelievably, in the final chukka, Churchill scored yet again. Time ran out and the Hussars had won. However, the victory was to be their last, as many of the players would perish in the coming war, and the team would never play together again. Churchill called polo 'the prince of games'.

Politics: Crowded Halls

Churchill left the army in the spring of 1899, returned to England and attempted to win a seat as a Conservative Unionist in the working-class marginal constituency of Oldham, Lancashire. Amid packed town halls, fervent speeches, political blustering and heated meetings the result was a swing to the Radicals by 2 per cent — Churchill remembered it as a great experience. In a poll of 23,000 votes, he trailed the Liberal candidate by 1,300 votes.

Sailing to the Boer War: 'In Love with Words'

Trouble had been brewing in South Africa since the discovery of gold in Witwatersrand in 1886. The Boer (Dutch) Republics of Orange Free State and Transvaal deeply resented the influx of British pioneers and speculators. Their president, Paul Kruger, vehemently opposed these 'Uitlanders' and presented the British, mainly in Natal and Cape Province, with an unacceptable ultimatum. War was declared on 12 October 1899. Churchill had already made plans; *The Morning Post* had commissioned him for a four-month assignment at £250 per month plus all expenses to cover the war and send back campaign stories. He sailed on the *Dunottar Castle* on 14 October with his valet and sixty bottles of claret, port, vermouth and Scotch whisky. A journalist on board, J. B. Atkins of *The Manchester Guardian* noted, 'He was slim, slightly reddish-haired, pale, lively, plunging along the deck with neck out-thrust, sometimes in meditation.' He listened to Churchill. 'It was obvious he was in love with words. He would hesitate sometimes before he chose one or would change one for the better ... ambitious, unabashed, frankly egotistical ... no reverence for his seniors, [he] talked to them as though they were his own age or younger.'

Boer War: Ambushed

The story of Churchill's astonishing adventures in the Boer War was mainly told in his columns in *The Morning Post*, and subsequently in his *My Early Life*. After landing at the Cape he and Atkins spent four days travelling by steamer and rail on their way to Ladysmith, scene of the heaviest fighting. By the Natal railway they reached Estcourt. Here, by chance, they met Leo Amery (from Harrow days, when Winston, under the impression Amery was no older than himself, had pushed the sixth former into the swimming pool — a Harrovian crime) and Aylmer Haldane, whom Churchill had known in India. The latter, commanding the Dublin Fusiliers, invited him to join his armoured train along ten miles of rail towards Colenso. On the way, however, at Chieveley, the train was ambushed. Having rescued many of the wounded, Churchill was captured by the Boers. It was 15 November; on 13 December he escaped from Pretoria prison camp wearing a brown suit, with £75 in cash and four slabs of chocolate and 'jumped' a goods train. After various adventures he reached Lourenço Marques (a Portuguese coastal town) and caught another train to Durban where he was greeted as a hero. The Boers then offered a reward of £25 for 'an Englishman, 25 years of age, about 5 feet 8 inches in height, medium build, stooping gait, fair complexion, reddish brown hair, almost invisible slight moustache, speaks though his nose, cannot give full expression to the letter 's',

Above: Churchill had rendered himself liable to be shot as a civilian taking part in military operations. The Boers, however, were lenient and treated him as an ordinary prisoner-of-war. He planned to escape and release the 200 British prisoners in captivity nearby, and, if possible, capture Pretoria itself. His companions refused to consider this rash scheme. He therefore decided on a less ambitious, but still enterprising method of escape. He is the figure on the right in the cap, standing apart.

Below: A sketch of the camp from which Winston Churchill escaped. He was not a prisoner for very long. On 12 December he planned to escape with two comrades. He was the first to climb the enclosure and managed to elude the sentries. The other two were caught.

HOW I ESCAPED
FROM PRETORIA.

By Winston Churchill.

THE *Morning Post* has received the following telegram from Mr. Winston Spencer Churchill, its war correspondent, who was taken prisoner by the Boers and escaped from Pretoria.

LOURENCO MARQUES, December 21st, 10 p.m.

I was concealed in a railway truck under great sacks.

I had a small store of good water with me.

I remained hidden, chancing discovery.

The Boers searched the train at Komati Poort, but did not search deep enough, so after sixty hours of misery I came safely here.

I am very weak, but I am free.

I have lost many pounds weight, but I am lighter in heart.

I shall also avail myself of every opportunity from this moment to urge with earnestness an unflinching and uncompromising prosecution of the war.

On the afternoon of the 12th the Transvaal Government's Secretary for War informed me that there was little chance of my release.

I therefore resolved to escape the same night, and left the State Schools Prison at Pretoria by climbing the wall when the sentries' backs were turned momentarily.

I walked through the streets of the town without any disguise, meeting many burghers, but I was not challenged in the crowd.

I got through the pickets of the Town Guard, and struck the Delagoa Bay Railroad.

I walked along it, evading the watchers at the bridges and culverts.

I waited for a train beyond the first station.

The one 11.10 goods train from Pretoria arrived, and before it had reached full speed I boarded with great difficulty, and hid myself under coal sacks.

I jumped from the train before dawn, and sheltered during the day in a small wood, in company with a huge vulture, who displayed a lively interest in me.

I walked on at dusk.

There were no more trains that night.

The danger of meeting the guards of the railway line continued; but I was obliged to follow it, as I had no compass or map.

I had to make wide *detours* to avoid the bridges, stations, and huts.

My progress was very slow, and chocolate is not a satisfying food.

The outlook was gloomy, but I persevered, with God's help, for five days.

The food I had to have was very precarious.

I was lying up at daylight, and walking on at night time, and, meanwhile, my escape had been discovered and my description telegraphed everywhere.

All the trains were searched.

Everyone was on the watch for me.

Four wrong people were arrested.

But on the sixth day I managed to board a train beyond Middleburg, whence there is a direct service to Delagoa.

Above: Part of the article 'How I Escaped' published by *Pearson's Illustrated War News.*

Left: The reward notice for £25.

£25.—.—

(vijf en twintig pond stg.) belooning uitgeloofd door de Sub-Commissie van Wijk V voor den Specialen Constabel dezer wijk, die den ontvluchte Krijgsgevangene
     Churchill
levend of dood te dezen Kantore aflevert. —

Namens de Sub- Comm.
    wijk V
Oo de Haas
    Sec

Translation.

£25

(Twenty-five Pounds stg.) REWARD is offered by the Sub-Commission of the fifth division, on behalf of the Special Constable of the said division, to anyone who brings the escaped prisoner of war

CHURCHILL,

dead or alive to this office.

For the Sub-Commission of the fifth division,
    (Signed) LODK. de HAAS, Sec.

NOTE.—The Original Reward for the arrest of Winston Churchill on his escape from Pretoria, posted on the Government House at Pretoria, brought to England by the Hon. Henry Massey, and is now the property of W. B. Horton.

and does not know a word of Dutch. Wore a suit of brown clothes, but not uniform — an ordinary suit of clothes.' An amazingly accurate description of the fugitive from the Acting Commissioner of Police, Pretoria.

The Boers had swept down into Natal, routed and killed General Symonds, surrounded George White's troops in Ladysmith and won a convincing victory at Nicholson's Nek. To the west, Baden-Powell was besieged in Mafeking and further south Kimberley was under attack.

Boer War: Perfect Happiness

Churchill was now a national hero. Other correspondents and the wounded who had escaped the ambushed train were full of his gallant exploits. He was given a commission in the South African Light Horse, an irregular force with gaily plumed hats known as the 'Cocky-Ollie Birds'. As a journalist he could not rejoin the British Army, yet, bedecked with his badges of rank on his coat and the plume of the sakabulu bird in his hat, it was a time of perfect happiness for him.

'Terrible Scenes'

Churchill took part in the relief of Ladysmith. Next he joined Montmorency's Scouts, an Imperial Yeomanry unit. He took part in the disastrous battle of Spion Kop 20-22 January 1900, when the bumbling General Sir Redvers Buller's force suffered 1,500 casualties in the most horrific scenes he'd ever witnessed. His brother Jack was wounded at Spion Kop. Churchill saw further action at Hussar Hill, Potgieter's Ferry and Diamond Hill. He was amongst the first troops to enter and later rode, on a bicycle, into Johannesburg, which was still occupied by the Boers. By the first week of June, Churchill and his cousin, the Duke of Marlborough, on horseback, headed the first column into Pretoria and liberated their comrades from the POW camp. He resigned his (unpaid) commission ten days later. Lady Randolph joined her son briefly, having raised funds for, and travelled with, the hospital ship *Maine*. It was filled with wounded soldiers and she returned with it to England.

Churchill, at the age of twenty-five, had acquired fame through his exploits. He also was very well paid for his journalism and by the time he arrived back home in July had material for several books.

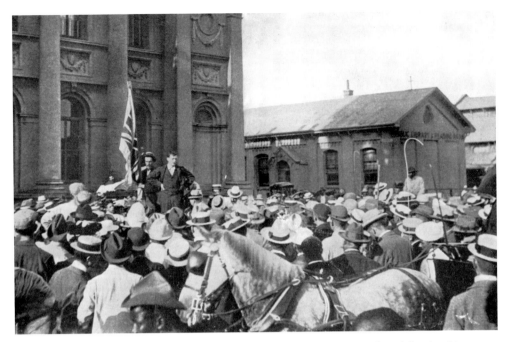

Winston Churchill addresses the crowd during his reception at Durban following his remarkable escape from the Boers.

In Durance Vile

Although the young Churchill was incarcerated by the Boers for only four weeks, it had a profound effect on him. He certainly hated every minute of his captivity more than he had ever hated any other period in his whole life. '... Prisoner of War! That is the least unfortunate kind of prisoner to be, but it is nevertheless a melancholy state. You are in the power of the enemy. You owe your life to his humanity and your daily bread to his compassion. You must obey his orders, go where he tells you, stay where you are bid, await his pleasure, possess your soul in patience.' In after years when Churchill was Home Secretary and had all the prisons of England in his charge he did his utmost, consistent with public policy, to introduce variety and indulgence into the life of the inmates, giving them books to mitigate their hard lot as far as was reasonable.

The Khaki Election

On the way back by sea from the Cape on the *Dunottar Castle*, Churchill finished writing *Ian Hamilton's March*, which appeared in October. *Savrola*

Later in the war
Winston Churchill
joined the South
African Light Horse,
the 'Cockyoli Birds'.

had been published in February. The Conservative Government called a General Election. His cousin, 'Sunny' Marlborough, offered Churchill his rooms at 105 Mount Street, London, which was his base for the next six years. Sunny also put up £400 to pay for Churchill's election expenses as he tried again for the Oldham constituency. The 'Khaki Election' in Oldham was a great and vibrant event. Joseph Chamberlain came to speak for him and he scraped home in second place behind Alfred Emmott, but was elected; from his time on his attendance at political events around the country was demanded. His second Boer War book, *From London to Ladysmith*, was also published in 1900 and his mother Lady Randolph married a young social butterfly of his own age — George Cornwallis-West.

'Chattering little Cad'

On 18 February 1900 Winston made his maiden speech and first met David Lloyd George in the House of Commons. Much later that year Lloyd George

MY CELEBRATED
LONG·BOW

THE IDENTICAL VULTURE

Above: Winston Churchill at the time of the Oldham election.

Right: A political cartoon by Edward T. Reed from *Punch* at the time of the Oldham election. During his escape from the Boers, Churchill recorded that throughout the night he was eyed by a vulture, and this imagary appears in numerous contemporary cartoons.

went to speak against the Boer War at Birmingham Town Hall. A huge, angry, jingoistic mob chased him away in the riot that followed. Winston commented, 'Personally I think Lloyd George a vulgar, chattering little cad, but he will have gained a hundred thousand sympathisers in England by the late proceedings.'

The Capitalist

In the three years spanning 1898 to 1900 Churchill had published no fewer than five books: The Story of the Malakand Field Force, *The River War*, his novel *Savrola*, and the two South African books: *From London to Ladysmith* and *Ian Hamilton's March*. He earned and then spent considerable amounts of money. To his mother, he wrote of how exceedingly proud he was of his financial achievements, and that few people in his position could have made as much money (around £10,000) without any prior capital. This large sum (perhaps half-a-million pounds today) he handed over to Sir Ernest Cassel, a close friend of King Edward VII, to invest. Churchill found Cassel's villa in Switzerland an agreeable bolt-hole for writing and for climbing the mountains of the Valais — though, ignominiously, he had to return from the Eggishorn on a mule.

The American Coincidence

In the spring of 1900 Winston Churchill of Windsor, Vermont, USA, wrote yet another bestselling novel, *Richard Carvel*, which would also sell well in the English market. Very politely the 'doppelgängers' sorted themselves out. British Churchill used the name 'Winston Spencer Churchill' for his books and articles. After *Savrola* he was not tempted to write another novel. In the year 1900 Churchill visited Boston where his namesake happily welcomed him, and at the banquet that followed both made flattering speeches about the other.

King Edward VII: 'Gadzooks'

Before taking his seat in Parliament, Churchill rode his luck and toured the UK, lecturing (chaired by VIPs) on his South African experiences, which earned him £3,782. Encouraged, he then sped off to America, met Mark Twain in New York, and in Winnipeg heard of the death of Queen Victoria. He wrote to his mother in January 1901 expressing his gladness that Edward now had his chance to sit on the throne; 'gadzooks' was his exclamation about how

A studio photograph of Winston Churchill taken in Boston during his 1900 tour.

long it was since the British throne had last seen an 'Edward'. He took his seat in Parliament on 14 February 1901 and made his maiden speech four days later. He followed a dynamic firebrand Welsh MP, a pro-Boer called Lloyd George. The next day *The Daily News* described it as 'A Kind of Duel'. His opportunism, ambition, lack of small talk and indifference to other people were clear to see and made him many enemies.

The 'Hughligans' or 'Hooligans' Coterie

Under Lord Hugh Cecil (the fifth son of the Marquess of Salisbury) a coterie of five young Conservative MPs became known as the 'Hughligans' in the period 1902–03: Earl Percy, the eldest son of the seventh Duke of Northumberland; Arthur Stanley, a younger son of the Earl of Derby; Ian Malcolm, a handsome debonair man (later to marry Lillie Langtry's daughter); and Churchill. They were all bachelors and were all linked to Arthur Balfour, the then Prime Minister. They were a small, independent and adventurous group who acted together on tactics and policy and dined together every Thursday in the subterranean private dining rooms of the House of Commons. They made themselves unpopular with the Front Bench of the Conservative Party who christened them 'The Hooligans'. They made a lot of noise, entertained all the key politicians of the day and achieved very little.

'The Jolly Little Trout'

Churchill liked the female sex but his social manner was not popular. Two enchanting dinner guests — Lady Horner (who found him morose and silent) said, 'I don't like people who make me feel as though I wasn't there,' and Diana Lister (later Lady Westmoreland) who was so angry at Churchill's absence of polite conversation that she rose from the table and continued her meal at the sideboard. Later he enquired 'What happened to that jolly little trout?' Only Violet Asquith put in a good word for him.

'Infant-School Economics'

Beatrice Webb and her husband Sidney were ardent social reformers and occasionally met Churchill. In July 1903 Beatrice described him in her diary: 'restless ... egoistical, bumptious, shallow-minded and reactionary, but with a certain personal magnetism, great pluck and some originality, not of intellect but of character ... Bound to be unpopular, too unpleasant a flavour with his restless self-regarding personality and lack of moral or intellectual refinement ... But his pluck, courage, resourcefulness and great tradition may carry him far unless he knocks himself to pieces like his father.' And, a year later: 'he drinks too much, talks too much and does no thinking worthy of the name ... still in the stage of "infant-school economics".'

The Blenheim Rat

Divine discontent soon set in. Churchill urged that the Boers be treated with generosity (not a popular sentiment). He criticized the Army Estimates and declared that the Royal Navy was Britain's sure defence (and needed more financial support). He spoke for and voted for Free Trade against Joseph Chamberlain's campaign for Tariff Reform. His two main themes in his speeches were on Army reform and on the economy. By early 1902 he was out of step with his Conservative front benchers, on one occasion leading a Tory back-bench revolt which voted with the Liberals. He mooted the idea of a 'Fourth Party', a central coalition 'Tory-Liberal' (as his father had done). He goaded

Winston delivered his maiden speech in the midst of the Boer War debate. He pleaded for a full account of the operations. 'I have in many cases myself supplied the only report given to the country on some important matter,' he said, referring to his correspondence in the *Morning Post*. He continued: 'I feel keenly the responsibility which has thus been placed upon me, and I think it is time for the Secretary for War to relieve me of some of it.' Whereupon Herbert Asquith spoke of 'that burden of responsibility that at present weighs so heavily on the honorable member's shoulders.' With this fine touch of irony, the Liberal leader found the weak place in Churchill's heart.

the Prime Minister Arthur Balfour on many occasions and caused cracks in the unity of his party. By 1904 he was detested by most of the Conservative MPs, seen as a traitor to his party and to his aristocratic class. On one occasion Balfour and eighty Tory MPs walked out of the Chamber during one of his speeches. It was a calculated insult. On 31 May 1904, he crossed the floor and took the corner seat below the Opposition gangway, next to Lloyd George, where his beloved father used to sit. He had earned a reputation for 'treachery' and also the nickname 'The Blenheim Rat'.

Mr Winston Churchill and Mr Balfour.
Mr Balfour: 'Confound the boy! He's always doing something weird!'
Westminster Gazette, February 1902.

Churchill became more Radical, and roused his Conservative fellows to fury. In March 1904 his close friend, Major Seely, resigned from the Conservative Party on the question of 'Chinese slavery' in South Africa. There was such an outcry that Major Seely could scarcely make himself heard, and Churchill shouted: 'I am quite unable to hear what my honourable Friend is saying owing to the vulgar clamour maintained by the Conservative Party.' At this, Sir George Trout Bartley shouted that 'the vulgarest expression came from this honourable Gentleman'. On 31 May 1904 Winston Churchill crossed the House and took his seat on the Liberal benches beside Lloyd George.

Winston's laugh was unlike anyone else's; it was infectious. At a public meeting he used to share in the merriment incited by his own jests, which did no harm to his popularity. In private life, however, there was no need to lend a helping grin. Everyone chuckled at his subtle and prematurely wise humour. No one else possessed Winston's facility for self-teasing. As a young man he never displayed the same humour twice, but always he was entertaining, good-natured, and encouraging to everyone.

'Henpecked': the 'Flapper' Vote

During the General Election of 13 January 1906 the suffragettes seeking their votes launched a militant campaign. In North-West Manchester Miss Sylvia Pankhurst and Mrs Drummond, two most formidable leaders of the noisy movement, concentrated their fire on Churchill. Night after night they demonstrated to try to wreck his meetings. Banners were unfurled, speeches interrupted, ejections took place as they caused considerable disorder. Churchill invited one of the suffragettes onto the platform and she asked, 'Will the Liberal Government give women votes?' She received a negative reply, although he admitted on the only occasion on which he had voted he had supported the pro-suffrage motion. But, he told his audience, he was not going to be henpecked. It became a popular catchphrase: 'Don't be henpecked, Winston.' Four years later as Home Secretary he gave orders that suffragettes in prison should be 'pampered'. In 1918 women over thirty were given the vote, and in 1928 women over twenty-one. Clementine Hozier, the woman Churchill would marry in 1908, was a keen supporter of the suffragettes.

Campaigning as a Liberal for Manchester North West during the general election of 1906. He won the seat with a majority of 1,214 votes and represented the constituency for two years. When Campbell-Bannerman was succeeded by Herbert Asquith in 1908, Churchill was promoted o the Cabinet as President of the Board of Trade. Under the law at that time he was obliged to seek re-election, but lost his seat. He was soon back in Parliament representing Dundee.

'Grand Slam in Doubled No-Trumps'

On 9 December 1905, Sir Henry Campbell-Bannerman, the Liberal Party Prime Minister, offered his distinguished young 'convert' the Financial Secretaryship of the Treasury, a senior post which ought to lead to the Cabinet. Churchill instead asked for Under-Secretary for the Colonies, where he would have less supervision, as the Secretary of State, Lord Elgin, sat in the House of Lords. But a few weeks later another General Election was held and in North-West Manchester as in the rest of the country the Conservatives were routed — all nine Conservative seats were, on the morning of 13 January 1906, now held by the Liberals.

Mr Charles Hands, a *Daily Mail* journalist known to Churchill from the Boer War days, was asked to supper. 'What did you think of that?' (The election result.) Churchill was said to have replied that 'it was a grand slam in doubled no-trumps.' His own majority was 1,241 in a 10,000 vote. A close friend, Lord Hugh Cecil, had warned him that to succeed as a minister 'requires a reputation as a good administrator, a skilled and industrious official' — good advice indeed.

A *Punch* cartoon from 1907; 'One Step Nearer'. Towards the middle of April 1907, Under-Secretary Churchill became a Privy Councillor.

Lord Randolph Vindicated

Macmillan published Churchill's magisterial two-volume biography of his father on 1 January 1906. His agent was the notorious Frank Harris (author of *My Life and Loves*). In the first four months 6,000 copies were sold and a royalty advance of £8,000 was received. The book was much praised. Three years of research resulting in a 250,000-word book, handwritten by the author, would indubitably have made his father proud. Much of the research had been done at Blenheim Palace, where Sunny Marlborough, who had most of Lord Randolph's papers, kept several rooms open for Churchill — and put good hunters at his disposal during the winter.

Royal Correspondence

Quite often in 1905–06 Churchill wrote directly to King Edward VII on matters connected with the Empire that he deemed to be important. From Baron de Forest's magnificent steam yacht he sent his monarch a 35-page handwritten document about the Transvaal's request for self-government. Answers came back via private secretaries or the Prime Minister. One ended, 'His Majesty is glad to see that "you are becoming a *reliable* minister and above all a *serious* politician."'

'Kaisermanoeuvre'

In September 1906 Kaiser Wilhelm II of Germany invited Churchill, as Britain's Colonial Under-Secretary, to be an honoured guest at the German Army 'Kaisermanoeuvre' to be held at Breslau in Silesia. Before he went, King Edward VII sent Churchill, via Campbell-Bannerman, the PM, a clear message 'to warn you against being too communicative and frank with his nephew [the Kaiser]. I have no doubt you will, as the penny-a-liners [tabloid press] say "Exercise a wise discretion".' Wearing his uniform as a major in the Oxfordshire Yeomanry, Churchill duly attended on horseback the mock battles, enjoyed the full-dress banquets and operatic performances that followed. Not only the whole German court, but also many important foreign guests, attachés, ministers and generals attended. On the way to Breslau, he visited Deauville where he gambled every night till the early hours of the morning — and suffered for his social exertions. He won £260 (about £12,000 currently).

A *Punch* cartoon from 1906; Churchill advising the Kaiser Wilhelm II after the German Army Manoeuvres.

Winston Churchill with Kaiser Wilhelm II.

The East African 'Progress'

In the autumn of 1907, Churchill, as Under-Secretary of State at the Colonial Office under Lord Elgin, was much involved in the granting of self-government to the Transvaal and the Orange Free State. In West and East Africa he opposed any military actions, advocating imperial control and greater railway development. He decided to make an African progress by sea to East Africa ostentatiously as a sporting and private expedition. He intended to work fourteen hours a day (much of it on well-paid articles for *The Strand Magazine*). His slogan was 'sofari so goodly'; the safari lasted four months. By foot, on bicycle, rickshaw, motor car, canoe and a steamer from Mombasa, he travelled to Victoria Nyanza, to Lake Albert and north up the Nile to Khartoum and Cairo. He hunted lions, shot a white rhinoceros, admired the colourful butterflies, inspected possible railway routes, infuriated the Governors and their staff and thoroughly enjoyed himself.

Rock-climbing: Exciting, Serious and Important

Violet Asquith was a young woman of great character. She persuaded Churchill up to Aberdeenshire where he 'flung himself with zest into our favourite and most perilous pastime of rock-climbing, revelling in the scramble up crags and cliffs, the precarious transition from ledge to ledge, with slippery sea-weed underfoot

Winston with David
Lloyd George.

Winston with his
mother Jennie, Lady
Churchill.

and roaring seas below ... He always took command of every operation, decreeing strategy and tactics and even dictating the correct position of our arms and legs. He brought to every ploy the excitement of a child and, like a child, he made it seem not only exciting but serious and important.'

The Gambler

Churchill gambled at many casinos in France, particularly on the French Riviera and at Monte Carlo, while with his coterie of Oxfordshire Hussars he gambled heavily through the summer evenings, and on board the Admiralty yacht HMS *Enchantress* the golden court around him either danced or played cards. Clementine naturally did not approve although she too gambled at the tables for small stakes. At roulette Churchill nearly always played red; at bridge he was rash, impatient and made every kind of mistake. At bezique or mah-jong he was known to be an erratic scorer: his arithmetic was rather haphazard. He once held off drinking brandy for a year for a large bet. And his post-war horse-racing activities demanded bets and punts!

'Sulky' Irish Catholics

In the by-election for North-West Manchester held in April 1908 Churchill was defeated, to the glee of the Tory Party. A few days earlier he had been confident that the unpredictable elements of the voting population — the Jews, the Irish and the Free Traders — would vote in his favour. But he had a swing of 6.6 per cent against him and blamed the loss on 'sulky' Irish Catholics. Despite his defeat, however, the Liberal Party stood by him, and Churchill was grateful for their loyalty and kindness. He was offered a number of safe seats and at Dundee he was duly elected on 9 May and in Herbert Asquith's Government became President of the Board of Trade, aged thirty-three.

The Greek Ship

Clementine Hozier, aged nineteen, first met Winston Churchill at a fashionable London ball in the summer of 1904, when he was twenty-nine. She was the second child of Colonel Sir Henry Hozier and Lady Blanche (née Ogilvy). The colonel was a soldier, military attaché, author and finally Secretary to the Corporation of Lloyds of London. He died in 1907 and did not know Churchill. Lady Blanche for her part was distinctly promiscuous. Clementine

Clementine Hozier.

had had two very close admirers, to both of whom she had been engaged: Sidney Peel (fifteen years older than her, and grandson of the famous Sir Robert) and Lionel Earle (a wealthy civil servant, of 'good family' — and even older than Peel. Given the state of her parents' marriage, could she have been seeking a father figure?). In April 1908 Churchill met Clementine again at a dinner party given by Lady St Helier. She was described by Violet Asquith: '[a] face of classical perfection ... a profile like the prow of a Greek ship ... I gazed upon her finished, flawless beauty and reflected on her wide experience of the world ... Awe vanished, admiration stayed, and with it began a friendship which no vicissitude has ever shaken.'

That month the young lovers, Winston and Clementine, began a long, beautiful dialogue of letters that was to extend for half a century.

The Virginal Snowdrops

Churchill's grandmother, the Duchess of Marlborough, told him, 'It is clear you have not yet attained a Knowledge of Women — and it is evident you have (I am thankful to see) no experience of love.' Churchill was thirty-four when he married Clementine Hozier and his name had been linked — rather vaguely — with a number of pretty young women: Polly Hacket, Mabel Love, Muriel Wilson, Ethel Barrymore, Maxine Elliott and — more certainly — with Pamela Plowden. According to Violet Asquith, who was definitely much attached to him, 'His approach to women was essentially romantic.' She thought he divided women into two categories — 'the virginal snowdrops, unsullied by experience, or even knowledge, of the seamy side of life, who should be sheltered and protected from its hazards; and the mature who ... had scrambled in and out of pitfalls and adventures ... and it was amongst these that he sought — not his romances, but his female friends.'

The engagement of Clementine Hozier to Winston Churchill, 1908. He had proposed to Clementine at a house party at Blenheim Palace on 10 August 1908.

Blenheim Palace: A Proposal

By early August 1908, Churchill and Clementine's friendship deepened and she agreed to come to Blenheim Palace as part of a house party which included Lady Randolph (Jennie), the F. E. Smiths (the brilliant advocate, orator and Conservative MP and one of Churchill's closest friends) and Edward Marsh (Churchill's Private Secretary). Churchill wrote to Clementine, encouraging her to come by, describing the pleasures of Blenheim Palace: its rose gardens, pools, lakes, and the many and various treasures the palace housed. On 11 August, having been caught in a rain shower while walking the grounds, Churchill and Clementine took refuge in the little Temple of Diana overlooking the Great Lake. There, Churchill proposed marriage and was accepted.

'A Glorified Coachman'

About 1,300 guests attended the grand wedding of Winston and Clementine on 12 September 1908 at St Margaret's, Westminster. Bishop Edwards of St Asaph officiated, Dean Welldon of Manchester (Churchill's headmaster at Harrow) gave the address, Lord Hugh Cecil was best man and Lloyd George signed the register. The *Tailor and Cutter* rather unkindly described Churchill's clothes as 'one of the greatest failures as a wedding garment ... a sort of glorified coachman appearance'. This was not fair as the wedding photographs show an immensely dapper, youngish man with topper, frock-coat and a wide grin. The bride wore diamond earrings (Churchill's present), a lustrous white satin gown, a flowing veil of soft tulle and a tiara of orange blossom. She was given away by her brother Bill Hozier. After a honeymoon in Italy, they set up home in Churchill's refurbished bachelor flat in Bolton Street, and the next year — 1909 — moved to Eccleston Square.

'More Than a Phrase-monger'

Beatrice and Sidney Webb lunched with Winston and Clementine Churchill on 10 October 1908. This time, four years since their first meeting, Beatrice changed her acerbic views: 'Winston C and his bride — a charming lady, well-bred and pretty and earnest with it, but not rich, by no means a "good match", which is to Winston's credit.' Winston had made a really eloquent speech on the unemployed the night before and he had mastered the Webb scheme [Labour exchanges]. 'He is brilliantly able — more than a phrase-monger, I think.' She compared Churchill favourably with Lloyd George.

The wedding day, 12 September 1908. The couple were married in St Margaret's, Westminster.

The couple spent their honeymoon at Highgrove House in Eastcote, Ruislip. The house was owned by Hugh and Eleanor Warrender, friends of Lady Churchill.

German Manoeuvres:
Great Advances

Churchill was again invited by the German Kaiser to attend the German Army manoeuvres held at Wurzburg in 1909. They were more practical, more soldierly than the glittering hordes of 1906, and far more up-to-date in their tactics. The large masses of infantry seen previously — so easily wiped out by artillery and machine guns — had vanished; artillery was no longer positioned in long lines, but placed where tactically advantageous. No wonder the French military observers looked serious and worried. Churchill noted that the atmosphere of the ceremony was dominated by a sense of powerful, strident and tireless machismo and fortitude; a deadly and devastating spectacle.

The Social Reformer

During twenty months of 1908–09, influenced by the two Fabians, Sidney and Beatrice Webb, by social surveys carried out by Seebohm Rowntree and Charles Booth, and by his own working-class constituency of Dundee, Churchill introduced several significant bills in Parliament. There were Acts that regulated coal industry working conditions; a Trade Boards Bill that prohibited sweated labour; unemployment insurance; and the creation nationally of Labour Exchanges. The National Insurance Act incorporating both unemployment and health benefits was finally enacted in December 1911. As President of the Board of Trade, Churchill was the driving force behind these reforms, although Lloyd George as Chancellor of the Exchequer took most of the credit and glory.

Dreams

In 1909 Churchill declared that he wanted things done. He wanted dreams, but dreams that were realisable. He wanted aspiration and discontent leading to a real paradise and a real earth in which men could live there and then and fulfil the destiny of the human race. He wanted to make life better and kinder and safer at that precise moment. Suffering was too close to him, misery too near and insistent, injustice too obvious and glaring, danger too present. Winston had met danger in India, Cuba and South Africa, but there was still much more peril to come.

Winston Churchill was equally progressive in his private life. The Home Secretary used his stately carriage only for official occasions. Citizen Churchill was one of the first residents of London to patronize the taxicab.

Lloyd George's Thumb

When Churchill entered Asquith's Liberal Party Government Cabinet as President of the Board of Trade, he immediately came under David Lloyd George's spell. Both Clementine and Violet Asquith (now Bonham Carter) agreed that he was 'completely under Lloyd George's thumb'. Moreover, Lloyd George, politically or otherwise, directed, shaped and coloured Churchill's mental attitude and his political course during the next few years: there was no doubt that he was the dominant partner.

Lloyd George was fascinated by a mind even more swift and agile than his own and by its fertility and resource. From the older Welshman Churchill learned of Radicalism. One was born in Blenheim Palace, the other in a small Welsh village. One thrilled to Imperial Glory and the might of the British Empire. The other was a little Englander. Churchill was extremely loyal to Lloyd George despite his belief that Lloyd George was indifferent to principles and scruples. At the Café Royal in late June 1911, Churchill gave Lloyd George dinner, where the Chancellor praised Clementine's virtues, beauty and her enriching effect on Churchill — thus cementing the two men's friendship even further.

This photograph features the bearded C. P. (Charles Prestwich) Scott, editor and proprietor of the *Manchester Guardian*. The other passenger is not clear, but appears to be Jack, Winston's brother.

Home Secretary and the Prisoners

Just after Asquith led the Liberals to their victory in January 1910, Churchill had published a 150-page booklet called *The People's Rights* which included some of his earlier speeches. This was followed by an urgent memorandum to the Cabinet demanding the abolition of the House of Lords, which received little or no support. On 1 February Asquith, in the South of France (a popular resort for Prime Ministers), offered Churchill promotion from the Board of Trade to the Irish Office. Churchill declined promptly but politely and asked for either the Admiralty or the Home Office. Perhaps to Churchill's surprise, the Prime Minister gave him the role of Secretary of State for the Home Department, at the tender age of thirty-six. He became one of the most humane of Home Secretaries. He visited Pentonville prison and was deeply moved by the plight of the boy prisoners, many of whom were in prison for sleeping rough — i.e. for being homeless. He refused to prohibit roller-skating by children on the London pavements: 'They shall have their little fun!' He planned for prisons to have libraries, entertainments and lectures to help educate and interest the prisoners. Yet Churchill found the pressure of regularly exercising his power of life or death over condemned prisoners draining. Nevertheless, and indeed just before leaving office, despite the protests of judges, he ordered a number of remissions of sentences.

Our artist has curiously few opportunities of attending Cabinet Councils, but, after a careful study of Mr Winston Churchills letter to his constituents about the '8' (Dreadnoughts) question, in which he light-heartedly castigates every axiom and argument of his dear colleagues, he feels sure that the above can be no inaccurate representation of what usually occurs when the Cabinet meets in council. Punch, 21 April 1909.

Petty Offenders

As Home Secretary in 1910 Churchill announced various reforms in the Prison Vote — particularly for petty offences. Each year 90,000 people went to prison in default of payment, and over 5,000 young lads under twenty-one were sent to prison each year for offences such as stone throwing, playing football in the streets, gambling or swearing. Churchill wanted noncustodial sentences, following his belief that at a young age offenders should be supported, disciplined and re-educated, rather than locked up. A century later and the problems are much the same.

The Bird of Paradise

Violet Asquith often wondered whether the people, 'these earnest, high-thinking and low-living men made head or tail of Winston. There is no doubt that his political performance left them dazzled — and blinking, sometimes with a vague mistrust. I think that to them he seemed a Bird of Paradise, of brilliant plumage and incalculable habits.'

Tonypandy

In November 1910 Winston Churchill, as Home Secretary, earned the hatred of the Trade Unions. Strikes were threatened on railways, docks and coal mines. Rioting broke out in the Rhondda valley coal mines round Tonypandy and strikers were flooding the mines. The local Glamorgan police were unable to maintain order and appealed for military support. Instead, Churchill sent 500 Metropolitan Police to quell the riots and promised a Board of Trade enquiry. Though the police were heavily stoned the strike ended. 'Tonypandy!' became a shouted taunt from his many critics.

The Sidney Street Affair

In mid-December 1910, police caught a gang of (supposed) Latvians tunnelling into a Houndsditch jeweller's shop. The robbers killed two policemen, wounded a third and escaped. The Home Office phoned Churchill in his bath on 3 January 1911 to say that the desperadoes were holed up in Sidney Street, Stepney. Churchill approved that a platoon of Scots Guards from the Tower of London should reinforce the police surrounding the barricaded house. He relates the story in his *Thoughts and Adventures*, referring to it as 'The Stepney Affair'. He and Eddie Marsh, his Private Secretary, were driven there, both top-hatted and Churchill in a fine astrakhan-collared overcoat. In the siege that followed three more policemen were killed or wounded. Then the building caught fire. The inmates were now doomed either to burn or face fusillades of rifles, pistols and shotguns. The fire brigade hurried to the scene, but Churchill

At the Sidney Street, Stepney, there was a sensational gun battle on 3 January 1911. A bullet went straight through Churchill's top hat. Somehow the house caught fire, but on Churchill's orders the fire brigade stayed away. The core members of the gang were identified as Latvian refugees. The supposed leader of the Houndsditch gang was identified by the press as 'Peter the Painter' — said to be the alias of one Peter Piaktov, a Latvian-born Bolshevik.

advised the firemen to let it burn for an hour, which they did. Eventually two charred bodies of 'Peter the Painter's' gang were found and perhaps one or two others escaped. The 'Siege of Sidney Street' provided a field day for the press and for Churchill's critics. He was so excited by his experience that his lisp was worse than usual when he was faced by his reproachful secretary at the Home Office, Charles Masterman: 'Now Charleth, don't be croth, it wath such fun.'

The Other Club: 'Rancour or Asperity'

Churchill and F. E. Smith Were both blackballed for membership of 'The Club' (Conservative dominated) so in 1911 they founded 'The Other Club' in opposition. It met fortnightly on Thursdays, when the House of Commons was sitting, in the Pinafore Room at the Savoy Hotel. Churchill was the de facto chairman and sat in the middle of the table, his back to the river Thames. Members included peers, MPs, military chiefs, press barons and authors. Rule No. 12 noted 'Nothing in the rules or intercourse of the Club shall interfere with the rancour or asperity of party politics.' If thirteen members attended, a large toy black cat was placed next to the Chairman. It was a great accolade to be invited to join 'The Other Club'. Sir Henry Strakosch, the Anglo-South African financier who in 1938 'saved' Churchill's portfolio of stocks and shares, was made a member. So too, in 1962, Churchill made Aristotle Onassis a member, another benefactor, who came twice and left the club well-endowed with champagne.

The Regency Rakes

King George V was crowned on 22 June 1911 and Churchill and his great friend F. E. Smith, both officers in the Oxfordshire Yeomanry, had their annual camp in the grounds of Blenheim Park. They were brigaded with the Buckinghamshire Yeomanry. Often the squadrons would gallop over the Downs or have a Field Day against the Berkshire Yeomanry. Churchill described to his wife how he and Jack led the squadrons at a fast pace, to the applause of the crowd, while the Berkshires struggled to keep up. According to Churchill, he had persuaded the commanding general to order the brigade — 1,200 men and horses — to gallop the length of Blenheim Park in 'brigade mass', something that he thought went 'awfully well'. There was heavy gambling and drinking in the hot evenings. The gamblers, beside Churchill and F. E. Smith, included Sunny, Duke of Marlborough, Neil Primrose (Lord Rosebery's son) and Fred Cripps (Stafford's brother). They tried to keep their gambling losses from their wives, who described them as 'the Regency Rakes'.

A month before Winston and Clementine were married, they were preceded by brother Jack, who married Lady Gwendoline Bertie, ("Goonie"), 8 August 1908.

Campaigning at Southport on behalf of a colleague, Churchill, rushing to the train, grabbed an old, worn hat, a relic of his early youth, which his square-set head had long outgrown. A photographer caught the pair on the beach, and asked permission to take the candidate's picture. No candidate has ever refused such a request. Winston smiled straight into the lens. Madame lowered her head, and smiled, rather embarrassed, at the sand. She tried to avoid the painful aspect of her husband's terrible hat. From that day onwards, little hats on a broad head became Churchill's trade-mark among cartoonists. At first he was a little angry about it. But later became aware of the value of a personal symbol, preferably an amusing one, for the popularity of a man in public life.

More like a Revolution than a Strike

The summer of 1911 produced an almost national strike. Dockers and railway workers, urged on by militant trade unionists, threatened to disrupt the entire distribution of food and vital supplies to maintain the life of the country. As Home Secretary, Churchill had to resolve this grave emergency. Serious riots took place in four or five towns and minor riots in twenty or more places. There were many attacks on railway stations and signal boxes. Telegraph and signal wires were cut, trains stoned and railway tracks vandalized. Churchill authorized the Army to deploy 50,000 troops on strike duty, to garrison stations, protect trains and railway lines. Two strikers were shot at Llanelli when troops defended a train. HMS *Antrim* was dispatched to Merseyside to show the strikers the Government was determined. Lloyd George negotiated a settlement on 20 August, but not before King George V had telegraphed to Churchill: 'Accounts from Liverpool show that the situation there is more like a revolution than a strike'; Churchill's response was that the strike would now be fought out. Predictably, his colleagues in the Liberal Party were horrified at his 'whiff of grapeshot', while the opposition Tories praised his decisive actions.

Agadir and the Panthers

On 1 July 1911 the German gunboat, *Panther*, arrived off the Moroccan port of Agadir, a move seen by both France and Britain as an attempt to turn the port into a German naval base on the Atlantic, and an act of intimidation of a country that France regarded as within its protection. This provocative act brought Europe to the brink of war. Lloyd George made it clear to the German Ambassador that if they intended war Great Britain would side with France. On 6 August Churchill wrote to his wife and quipped that the German *Panther* was to be matched by Britain's 'Little Panther' (Lloyd George). Churchill believed that the Germans would see sense and cease their ominous advance, while Britain's relationship with France was strengthened as a result of both nations' mutual distrust of the Kaiser.

Security of the Nation, and the Coffee Break

The Agadir crisis meant that Churchill was now a changed man. He had seen traces of German malevolence at the Kaiser's manoeuvres. The security of the British nation, particularly after the sinister strikes, occupied him more and

Initially, Winston Churchill did not see Germany as a threat until in July 1911 the German gunboat, *Panther*, sailed into the Moroccan port of Agadir. He saw German expansionism thereafter and concluded Germany meant to make war. On becoming First Lord, Churchill invited Fisher, who had retired, to become his unofficial adviser. Fisher pushed Churchill to convert the fleet to oil power and pointed out that oil was more efficient and cheaper. This *Punch* cartoon records the change-over.

more. He joined the Committee of Imperial Defence at the end of August 1911 and wrote his memorandum, *Military Aspects of the Continental Problem*. He postulated a full-scale war with a German, Austro-Hungary Alliance pitted against a French-British Alliance. Russia would be involved, probably attacked by Germany, who would advance initially to attack France, through Belgium. 'On the twentieth day of mobilization the French Armies will have been driven from the line of the Meuse and will be falling back on Paris and the South. On the fortieth day, Germany will be extended at full strain both internally and on her war fronts.' The British Army of 107,000 regulars would go immediately to France and a further 100,000 British troops from India should reach Marseilles on the fortieth day, when the French could hope to turn the tide. This memorandum was entirely Churchill's planning. In the event, the great Battle of the Marne took place between 6 and 10 September 1914, approximately forty days after French mobilization. It was an astonishingly accurate forecast. The British-French timetable of defensive manoeuvres even allowed for 'dix minutes d'arrêt pour café.'

Golden Journeys on HMS Enchantress

When Herbert Asquith hesitatingly offered him the post of First Lord of the Admiralty in November 1911, Churchill did not move into Admiralty House

*Scene—
Mediterranean,
on board the
Admiralty yacht
'Enchantress'
Mr Winston
Churchill: 'Any
home news?'
Mr Asquith:
'How can there
be with you
here?'*
Punch, 21 May
1913

(which required twelve servants) for another eighteen months. But during the first three peacetime years of his tenure he spent a total of eight months on the enchanting HMS *Enchantress*. This Admiralty yacht was the official perquisite of the First Lord and his Board. They had the right and duty to sail the seas on their official visits, a tradition dating back to 1664. A handsome ship built in 1903 of 3,800 tons with a crew of nearly 200, it was ideal for visiting dockyards, ports, naval ships, fleet manoeuvres and attractive harbours in the Mediterranean. On board there were champagne receptions, dancing through the night, gambling, bridge playing and discussions about the affairs of the world. The Asquiths and their friends were frequently aboard, and for Violet at least, 'The memory of those golden journeys in our enchanted ship can never fade.' In his book *The World Crisis*, Churchill recorded how his weekends were spent visiting Fleet positions at Portsmouth, Portland and Devonport, and the Flotilla at Harwich. He would dine with various officers and continually discuss matters of naval war.

Winston shows the Premier how to splice the main brace. Asquith took fright at Churchill's sweeping changes and was afraid of the fanatic zeal which his own choice plunged into work. Churchill invited his chief aboard the Admiralty yacht *Enchantress* and explained to the Prime Minister the inner workings of the Navy. Invisibly Mr Punch sat in!

In October 1911 Winston Churchill was appointed First Lord of the Admiralty.

Being enthusiastic about all forms of endeavour, Winston Churchill followed the progress of the flying machine with interest. He and Clementine are pictured here at Hendon, October 1910.

New Car, a Submarine Dive, the Light Fantastic and Four Stags

Between 1911 and 1913 Churchill enjoyed a wide variety of activities other than politics or writing. He purchased a new red car for £610, a 15-20 Napier, which brought him much delight and excitement, for a tour in Scotland. He took King George V and his son Prince Albert (later King George VI), then aged seventeen, for a two-mile dive in a submarine, and found the young prince familiar with and unfazed by the submersible vehicle. In the same year — 1912 — he wrote to Clementine from Knebworth House (the Hertfordshire home of the Earl of Lytton, who had married Pamela Plowden). He had taken dancing lessons from the pretty little Miss 'Park Palings', and found himself surprised at his aptitude at the three-step — even so far as to suggest that he and friends should form a club, with trained teachers, so as to improve and enjoy such activities further. The next year, on 20 September, he stayed with the

Churchill at army manoeuvres, 1912. He continued to retain a keen interest in the army. General French is standing on Churchill's left, next to the umpire with the white armlet.

King at Balmoral Castle, where he hunted stags. This was Churchill's annual ministerial visit, and relations with the King were cordial and close.

H. H. Asquith on Churchill: 'Lightning in the Brain'

'I can't help being fond of him; he is so resourceful and undismayed: two of the qualities I like best.'

'He has no personal following, he is always hankering after coalitions and odd groupings, mainly designed to bring in F. E. Smith or perhaps the Duke of Marlborough. I think his future one of the most puzzling enigmas in politics.'

'He will never get to the top in English politics with all his wonderful gifts, to speak with the tongues of men and angels and to spend laborious days and nights in administration is no good if a man does not inspire trust.'

Neptune's ally. The First Lord of the Admiralty calls in a new element to redress the balance of the Old. *Punch*, 25 March 1911.

'He (once) declared that a political career was nothing to him in comparison with military glory ... He is a wonderful creature with a curious dash of schoolboy simplicity. What someone said of genius "a zigzag of lightning in the brain".'

Intrepid Airman

Early in 1913, Churchill, fascinated by the idea of flying, commenced instruction with Commander Spenser Grey and then with Lieutenant Jack Sedden RN. At that time the Royal Navy possessed a dozen aircraft, mainly Short 100s, and accidents were frequent. The planes were frail, their engines unreliable and each manoeuvre in the air was worked out by trial and error. Churchill claimed to have invented the terms 'seaplane' and 'flight' (for a group of four aircraft). He flew with many instructors including Gustav Hamel, a world-famous monoplane pilot. Group-Captain Scott (also Churchill's private secretary) usually took off and landed, but Churchill flew quite long distances in control of the plane; however he never became a *qualified* pilot.

In October at the Isle of Sheppey Naval Air Station Churchill went for a cruise in the Astra-Torres airship around Chatham and the Medway — he piloted the vessel for an hour. His main aviator was Charles Samson. Within a year he had become a much more experienced pilot, flying in high winds, and in many different types of aircraft; however, and perhaps more importantly, this experience gave him a great sense of the dangers, and affinity with the joys,

A contemporary caricature from *Punch*. Churchill had a course of flying lessons while he was First Lord of the Admiralty and came close to graduating as a pilot but, despite personal enthusiasm, he did not persevere with the instruction.

It is not known why Churchill did not continue, but there is conjecture that the pressure was from Clementine after Lieutenant G. V. Wildman-Lushington, his instructor, was killed in a flying accident at the end of 1913.

of flying. He felt personally invigorated and emboldened by his experiences as a pilot. At the outbreak of war, the British Navy was the only fleet in the world to have an air force of over a hundred planes, giving the fleet and coastal defences air protection.

The Dunkirk Circus

In 1913 Churchill began to form the Royal Naval Division (the RND) consisting of three brigades — the Marines, the Naval Volunteer Reserve and the Fleet Reserve (which included Rupert Brooke, the poet). Apart from the Marines, the private army consisted of a green, raw, but enthusiastic mixture of stokers, sailors, scholars, musicians, bus drivers, even poets. Churchill's 'Private Army' never fought at sea, but were at the disposal of the Admiralty. During 1914 Dunkirk was their base, which included squadrons of armoured Rolls-Royce cars and a naval air squadron. On 3 September Lord Kitchener, Commander-in-Chief of the British Army, agreed that the Royal Naval Air Service (the RNAS) should undertake the air defences of Britain. Churchill's 'Dunkirk Circus' sent out raiding sorties — miniature expeditionary forces to harass the German Zeppelin sheds at Cologne and Friedrichshafen and carry out aggressive activities in Belgium, at Ypres, Lille, Tournai and Douai using planes or armoured cars. A force of 3,000 Marines took Ostend and alarmed the Germans, who were convinced there were 40,000 'invaders'. The RNAS claimed to have destroyed six Zeppelins on the ground. The service's favourite song was:

> *So there we were a merry crew*
> *Winston Churchill's Army*
> *Hyde Park talkers*
> *Swell shopwalkers*
> *Cooks and waiters*
> *Wearing gaiters*
> *Good ole Palace Army.*

A Mad World

A few weeks before Austria declared war on Serbia in July 1914, then Germany on Russia and finally on France, Churchill sent the Naval Grand Fleet from Portland north to the Orkneys and Scapa Flow, thus dominating the North Sea. The French would help control the Mediterranean. Clementine and their three small children, Diana, Randolph and Sarah, were on holiday at Cromer. Churchill wrote despairingly to Clemmie about Germany's declaration of war on Russia; it appeared to him that the world had gone mad. Yet, as always, he would close the letter with an expression of his love and affection for her. On 4 August 1914 the Germans invaded Belgium and once again the anarchy of the situation hit Churchill hard; he wrote of 'catastrophe' and 'collapse', and the vagaries and unpredictability of war. That month Churchill's Navy had the responsibility of shipping the British Regular Army of seven divisions, 'The Old Contemptibles', across the Channel into the battle of Mons.

SIGINT: the Fabergé Eggs

Signals Intelligence (SIGINT) was housed, during the Great War, in Room 40 in the Admiralty Old Building. By good fortune the Imperial German Navy SKM (*Signal Kaiserliche Marine*) code book, and the HVB (German Admiralty codes for communicating with their merchant ships) and the VB (the last of the three vital code books) were obtained. The Russian Naval Attaché personally presented the SKM cipher to Churchill in London — 'a gift more precious than a dozen Fabergé eggs ...'

The 'Cocoa Press' was a term invented by Leo Maxae, editor of the *National Review* in relation to three London Radical newspapers; the *Daily News*, the *Morning Leader*, and the evening *Stir*. A large proportion of the shares of these newspapers were owned by the Cadbury family. The cartoon by Sidney Strube appeared in the *Daily Express*, 13 December 1913. Note Churchill's tiny hat in the cartoon.

The Stormy Friendship

Churchill had first met Admiral John Arbuthnot 'Jacky' Fisher at Biarritz in 1907. The two men got on, despite a difference in age of thirty-four years, and carried on an eccentric correspondence over the next few years. In his stormy six years (1904-10) as First Sea Lord, Fisher had created the British battle fleet, but he had a poor opinion of the Army and its commanders. *His* Navy ruled the seas and he objected to any continental campaigning of any kind. On his retirement he was promoted Admiral of the Fleet and in 1912 was appointed chairman of a royal commission on oil fuel in relation to the Navy. The Prime Minister had put Churchill into the Admiralty for two main reasons — to transport the British

Expeditionary Force safely across the Channel to support the French in case of a continental war; and to create a naval War Staff. Churchill appointed Admiral Jellicoe to be second in command of the Home fleet and then brought in Admiral Beatty as his Naval Secretary. Fisher approved. Then Churchill appointed to naval command three admirals of whom Fisher strongly disapproved. 'You have betrayed the Navy,' he said, packed his bags and withdrew, hurt, to Naples. Churchill invited Asquith to come for a Mediterranean cruise on the Admiralty yacht, *Enchantress*, and jointly they persuaded the difficult Fisher to return to his duties. But the drama escalated during the Dardanelles campaign.

Rat-Watching

At the outbreak of war Lloyd George described Churchill at the Admiralty 'like a dog sitting on the Dogger Bank looking at a rat poking his nose out of the hole at the other side of the water' — waiting to pounce on the German Navy.

John Bull: *I thought I had given you plenty, but if you really want more I suppose you must have it*. Churchill threatened to resign and there were rumours he would re-join the Conservatives. After Winston knocked a million pounds off his Naval estimates the Liberals let the Bill pass. *Westminster Gazette*, 4 March 1914.

Tory Chorus: "*You made me love you; I didn't want to do it.*" The Conservatives did not like the Naval expenditure any more than the Liberals did, but in the face of German aggression they were forced to comply. "You Made Me Love You" was a popular song hit at the time. *Punch*, 14 January 1914.

The Siege of Antwerp

Churchill knew that the Channel ports were vital to both sides, and recognized that Antwerp was now a thorn in the side of the German High Command. On 7 September 1914 the Kaiser ordered its capture at all costs and three weeks later the German Army was bombarding the defending forts with 17-inch howitzers. Four days later King Albert of the Belgians sent out urgent demands for help. A conference was held in Lord Kitchener's house with Sir Edward Grey, Churchill and others. The British minister in Antwerp, Sir Francis Villiers, thought that Antwerp might hold out for five days as the Belgian Government prepared to leave the city for Ostend. Churchill was then sent post-haste to see for himself what needed to be done to restore the situation. Two of his Naval Brigades embarked on 3 October. The Marine Brigade had already arrived.

The Very Rash Offer

Churchill appeared at the Antwerp HQ in the uniform of an Elder Brother of Trinity House (as First Lord of the Admiralty, he was entitled to the post of Elder Brother of this ancient organization, responsible for ensuring the safety of marine vessels round the British Isles, by means of lighthouses and other markers). He persuaded the Belgian King and Prime Minister to hold out for another ten days and reorganized the ailing defences, moving around in a cloak and yachting cap. He was enjoying himself so much that on 5 October he telegraphed Asquith proposing to resign as First Lord and take over command of the armed forces in Antwerp — with the appropriate rank. This rash offer was, of course, refused. General Henry Rawlinson, appointed to command the British IV Corps (including the 7th Division and the Cavalry Division), arrived on 7 October and Churchill wisely returned to London. Clementine gave birth to Sarah that day. Rupert Brooke wrote, 'Antwerp that night was like several different kinds of Hell — the

Kladderadatch, a German satirical newspaper views Winston's battle with U-Boats.

broken houses and dead horses lit by an infernal glare.' On 7 October the naval division made a thirty-mile march to the south, having lost 2,800 casualties in the battle. The battle of Antwerp gave a week to strengthen the defences of Dunkirk and Calais, but Churchill was heavily criticized for his role in the affair.

The Ark for Writers and Charmers

Theresa, Lady Londonderry, the colourful wife of the 6th Marquess (a cousin of Churchill), established, during the First World War, an exclusive dining club of the rich and famous called 'The Ark' — a refuge from the trauma of war outside. Fanciful names were given to all the members. She was 'Circe the Sorceress', Neville Chamberlain 'Neville the Devil', Stanley Baldwin 'Bruin the Bear' and Churchill 'Winston the Warlock'. Lady Theresa described The Ark as 'a salon where stage and star met statesmen, Liberals and Conservatives, writers and charmers' who 'all scratched, pinched and bit each other jocularly or argued fiercely together — but all answered to their names.' A couple of years after the war was over Churchill was left a substantial legacy in the will of his long-dead great-grandmother, Frances Anne, Marchioness of Londonderry, two heirs having died.

'Indescribable Relief to the Admiralty'

The Royal Navy had an unsatisfying start to the Great War. In August 1914 they failed to bring to battle in the Mediterranean the powerful warships *Goeben* and *Breslau*, which took refuge in Constantinople. In the next month three British cruisers, the *Aboukir*, *Hogue* and *Cressy* were sunk off the Dogger Bank, and in October the dreadnought *Audacious* was sunk by a German mine off the Irish coast.

The First Sea Lord, Prince Louis of Battenberg, a dedicated and loyal person but of German birth (who was soon to anglicize his name to Mountbatten), was victimized by the press and the public, so Churchill reluctantly accepted his resignation. When he brought the unpredictable seventy-three-year-old Lord Fisher back as First Sea Lord it brought a great sense of relief to the Admiralty. They all knew the tough old sea-dog, but knew little about Churchill. Almost immediately came the naval disaster at Coronel. The *Good Hope* and *Monmouth* were lost with all hands. But Lord Fisher organized the Navy's revenge and, at the Falklands, Admiral von Spee's five-cruiser squadron was sunk. However, when on 14 December the German fleet bombarded Hartlepool, Yarmouth, Whitby and Scarborough, the Navy's reputation suffered.

Achievement at the Admiralty: Toasting der Tag

In the four years that Churchill spent at the Admiralty, often, not always, supported by the formidable Jacky Fisher, he was responsible for many significant achievements. He improved conditions and pay of naval ratings; reformed naval discipline; and introduced new training schemes for warrant and petty officers. He also authorized a complete change-over from British coal to foreign oil, which increased the speed of all ships, was more economical, reduced the time for refuelling and the need for the dirty, fatiguing labour of intensive stoking. He then negotiated, in 1913, a contract with the Anglo-Persian Oil Company, which, for a cost of £10 million, safeguarded supply and gave the British Government a controlling share in that company. The largest naval guns were increased in size from 13.5-inch shell to 15-inch — a significant advantage over the opposition. He increased the naval estimates from £39 million annually to over £50 million, which helped pay for five new fast battleships; built with the new 15-inch guns; they had a speed of 25 knots and were protected by 13 inches of armour. Churchill wanted to maintain a 60 per cent superiority over the German Navy, so increased the construction of new battleships from two a year, to four, then five, thus greatly upsetting Kaiser Wilhelm; though, as Churchill was to write in *The World Crisis*, in his view the British Navy was a necessity while the German one was more a luxury. Across the water Alfred von Tirpitz (Secretary of State for the German Imperial Navy)

Prince Louis of Battenberg, here seen in 1914 on Horse Guards Parade with Winston Churchill, was of German origin and bore a German title. As First Sea Lord he had shared with Churchill the responsibility for keeping the fleet mobilized up to the outbreak of war. This was not known generally, and his origin was enough to start against him ill-informed murmurings which led to his retirement.

Admiral of the Fleet, John Arbuthnott "Jacky" Fisher, 1st Baron Fisher of Kilverstone, (1841-1920). He first officially retired from the Admiralty in 1911 on his 70th birthday, but became First Sea Lord again in 1914, but resigned seven months later in frustration over the Gallipoli campaign.

went on building warships as fast as he could and his officers toasted *der Tag* nightly.

The Three Naval Campaign Plans

The British Army had suffered a million casualties in the first three months of war — Churchill wrote to Asquith on 29 December 1914 deploring how the Allied Armies were being sent to their deaths, chewing on barbed wire — was there no alternative? He, Lloyd George and Maurice Hankey (President of the Cabinet secretariat) each separately produced plans to outflank the deadly killing grounds of the trench warfare of the Western Front. Churchill's plan was to dominate the Baltic, seize Borkum and Sylt, threaten the Kiel Canal and invade Schleswig Holstein, thus enabling Russia to land troops and capture Berlin. Lloyd George's plan was for an expedition to Salonika in northern Greece. Hankey's plan was to attack Turkey, force the Dardanelles, intimidate Constantinople and 'persuade' the Turkish Government to sue for peace. Then a fleet would intrude into the Sea of Marmara and probably Greece, Bulgaria and Romania would come into the war on the Allied side. Churchill read Hankey's paper and, on 31 December, wrote to the Prime Minister, stating that he, Lloyd George and Hankey were in agreement — Gallipoli would be attacked. Ironically, it was Hankey's plan that, put into action, caused an appalling disaster and Churchill's downfall.

Bombardment as a Token

The British Navy chased the two German warships *Goeben* and *Breslau* across the Mediterranean in August 1914 until they reached safety in Constantinople. There they were nominally sold to the Turks, who used their 'purchase' to bombard the Russian Black Sea ports of Odessa, Nikolaev and Sevastopol in November. Turkish Army forces were threatening the Caucasus. The Grand Duke Nicholas of Russia sent Lord Kitchener an urgent message on 2 January 1915. The Russians wanted immediate help. Kitchener sent a guarded message back via the British Ambassador in Petrograd that 'a demonstration' would be made against the Turks. The chance that Russia would collapse and release vast German Armies from the Eastern Front to fight on the Western Front, and thus overwhelm the Allied forces, could not be risked. Marshal Joffre, commanding the French Army, and Field Marshal Sir John French, commanding the British, were adamant that they could not weaken their positions. On 13 January Churchill ordered the bombardment of the Dardanelles forts as a 'demonstration', from a safe distance of 12–14,000 yards. It was a token gesture and at a conference Vice Admiral Sir Sackville Carden (commanding the Mediterranean fleet) was asked whether the Dardanelles could be forced by the Navy alone. His cautious answer was affirmative — given 'extended operations with large numbers of ships'. On 12 January he sent a detailed plan of attack to the Admiralty and on 19 February attacks by the Navy continued sporadically on the Turkish forts.

Dardanelles Naval Attack: Open Door?

Admiral de Robock's powerful fleet of British and French battleships and cruisers entered the Straits of the Dardanelles on 18 March. The Turkish forts near Chanak and Kalti Bahr were bombarded for half an hour. Then the French squadron moved in to continue the bombardment at a closer range. Soon, one British and two French ships were seriously damaged and the French *Bouvet* blew up and sank in two minutes. The so-called minesweepers (trawlers) that were sent in to clear the minefields came under fire and fled. Almost immediately *Inflexible*, *Irresistible* and *Ocean* were mined and sank with heavy casualties. Admiral Sir John de Robeck had lost six of his nine battleships deployed in the attack. 'It had been a disastrous day,' he recorded, although Churchill was more bullish, believing that had the Navy pushed through the bay once more it could have broken the Turkish defences. Afterwards Enver Pasha, the Turkish Minister of War, corroborated this belief, that 'If the English had only the courage to rush more ships through the

Dardanelles, they could have got to Constantinople, but their delay enabled us [the Turkish Army with German military advisers] thoroughly to fortify the Peninsula and in six weeks' time we had taken down there over 200 Austrian Skoda guns.' De Robeck sent a telegram to Churchill in London to say that he could not move again without military support. On 13 May Admirals Fisher, Wilson and Jackson overruled Churchill. The naval attack was over.

The Nobility of Youth

The young poet, Rupert Brooke, was one of Churchill's untrained but enthusiastic reservists in his 'Private Army', the RND. Brooke survived the ill-fated battle of Antwerp but later, on a French hospital ship in the Dardanelles, died of blood poisoning and was buried by his friends at night under a clouded moon, on the island of Skyros. Churchill had met Brooke twice and wrote of him in *The Times* of 26 April 1915, praising eloquently the poet's voice that spoke of the nobility of the youth who carried arms, and of the rightness of his nation's cause.

The Caterpillar System

The German Army soon learned how to protect its airfields on the French and Belgian coasts from Churchill's marauding 'Dunkirk Circus'. They mined and cratered the main roads, so there was a need for a cross-country armoured vehicle. Early in 1915 Churchill wrote to Asquith detailing his idea for just such a machine. Steam tractors, fitted with bullet-proof coverings inside which men and weaponry could be housed, would be relatively straightforward and quick to manufacture. Utilizing 'caterpillar tracks' — rigid units joined to each other in a continuous belt that distributes the weight of a vehicle over a greater area than would otherwise be the case — would, Churchill suggested, allow the vehicle to cross the rugged terrain and trenches of the battlefield, crushing in its path the German barbed-wire defences. This was the first step in the practical evolution of the tank, which at the battle of Cambrai helped win the Great War.

Dardanelles: 'I'm Finished ... I'm Done'

'Never reinforce failure' is a well-tried military maxim that was now ignored. The immediate need to reinforce Russia had receded. Amidst confusion, inadequate staff preparations, faulty intelligence, inter-service rivalry and

The Mark I Tank was a tracked vehicle developed by the Army and entered service in August 1916. It was first used on 15 September 1916 during the Battle of Flers-Courcelette, of the Somme Offensive. It was the first vehicle to be named "tank", as a method of maintaining secrecy and disguising its true purpose.

non-cooperation, a new operation of amphibious landings went ahead. On 25 April (five weeks after the unsuccessful naval attack) a huge armada of 200 ships landed 30,000 British, Australian and New Zealand troops on the Gallipoli beaches, now well garrisoned and guarded. Two days of intensive fighting followed with very heavy losses on both sides. Bitter prolonged trench warfare followed. Churchill confided then to Violet Asquith: 'I'm finished ... I'm done. What I want above all things is to take some active part in beating the Germans ... I'd go out to the Front at once.' On 15 May the erratic, volatile Lord 'Jacky' Fisher resigned — again. Churchill's old friend Sir Ian Hamilton was now Commander-in-Chief of the Mediterranean Expeditionary Force. On 6 August another major attack was launched and failed with heavy losses. The Turkish defenders were brave and were 'advised' by experienced German officers. By the autumn the awful casualties on both sides produced a stalemate. Between December 1915 and January 1916 the British and Anzac Army was evacuated. To Churchill it was clear that Lord Fisher's sulphurous behaviour had totally betrayed him.

Death ... Just an Incident

Lord Kitchener asked Churchill on 17 July to visit the Dardanelles battleground to assess the situation there. It would have been a dangerous mission and Churchill made his financial affairs clear to Clementine, and, somewhat morbidly, entreated her not to grieve too much should he die. 'Death is just an incident' he told her. She should also guard his memory and look after the children. The event had a somewhat bathetic ending however; Tory ministers opposed and blocked the proposed visit.

'Through the Heart of Winston'

'The epic story of Gallipoli ... is one that I [Violet Asquith, daughter of the Prime Minister] cannot hope to tell dispassionately. I lived, through others, at its core. I saw it through the eyes and felt it through the heart of Winston, who conceived it, of my brother and close friends who fought on the Peninsula from first to last, of my father who believed in and supported it throughout. I shared with them its glories and its setbacks, its high hopes and the heartbreak of its final failure. Personal emotion may have blurred my vision, but I saw it then and see it still as the most imaginative conception of the First World War, and one which might, had all gone well, have proved the shortest cut to victory'

Clementine Votes for Winston's Future

Asquith had decided early in 1915 to form a national government — a coalition — and asked Churchill (then at the Admiralty) whether he would accept a place in the coalition or prefer a command on the Western Front. Clementine now vigorously defended Churchill and wrote directly to Asquith (whom she liked) on 20 May. She accepted that he (Asquith) and his colleagues might consider her husband to have faults, but asserted that he was almost alone among those same colleagues in having the power, imagination and deadliness to combat the German threat. Loyalty indeed!

'The Escaped Scapegoat'

Churchill appealed to everyone — Asquith, Bonar Law, Lloyd George — to no avail, and on 21 May he was offered the Chancellorship of the Duchy of Lancaster — a sinecure with no responsibility. He described himself as 'the escaped scapegoat'. When, on 15 November, the Dardanelles Committee was replaced by a War Committee he was excluded, and he resigned. As an MP he made an impassioned speech in the House of Commons: 'The essence of an attack upon the Gallipoli Peninsula was speed and vigour. We could reinforce from the sea more quickly than the Turks could reinforce by land ... To go slow, on the other hand — to leave long intervals between the attacks, so as to enable the Turks to draw reinforcements from their whole Empire ... was a great danger.' For the rest of his life Churchill was to suffer for the 'responsibility' for the Dardanelles failure. Lords Kitchener and Fisher certainly should have shared — equally — their sorry part in the disaster.

They were sad, desolate days for the Churchills. Clementine, overcome by grief, wept all the time.

The Muse of Painting

'Goonie', Lady Gwendoline, Churchill's sister-in-law, sketched in the gardens of Hoe Farm. Churchill was interested, picked up a box of watercolours belonging to one of the 'Kittens', made a few tentative experiments, ordered an easel, canvases, paints and brushes (May 1915). His first few efforts were interrupted by the arrival of Lady Hazel Lavery, the beautiful, audacious wife of the well-known Royal Academician, Sir John Lavery. She promptly took command, and taught him that boldness was all. So, with fierce strokes and decisive slashes of paint on canvas, his painting career was launched. Lavery remarked that Churchill 'would have made a great master of the brush'. In his book *Thoughts and Adventures* Churchill described the magic moment when he realized he had talent — it was as though the Muse of Painting came to his rescue.

Flanders Fields with the Grenadiers

In the House of Commons on 15 November Churchill made his long farewell speech, mainly, of course, about his record of the last fourteen months. The next day *en famille* at Jack Churchill's house, with Violet Asquith, Goonie, Eddie Marsh and others, he said another adieu. Violet said, 'For most of us it was a kind of wake.' On the 17th Max Aitken (Beaverbrook) called and found 'the soldier-statesman was buckling on his sword.'

On the 18th, Churchill, in the uniform of a major in the Queen's Own Oxfordshire Hussars, arrived in Boulogne to be taken to St-Omer to meet his old friend Sir John French, the Commander-in-Chief, who offered him command of a brigade; a month (with the Guards) would make Churchill 'master of the conditions of trench warfare'. Churchill joined the 2nd Battalion Grenadier Guards at Merville and received a cool reception from their Commanding Officer, Lieutenant-Colonel George Jeffreys. Churchill wrote to Clementine and described the gothic horror of the trenches — rubbish and filth everywhere, buried corpses reappearing through the soil, enormous rats skulking under the bright moonlight, and all around the whine of passing bullets — despite this awfulness, Churchill found happiness and contentment. It was at this time that he took to wearing a French steel helmet, which was the envy of his fellow soldiers.

Winston (through force of nautical habit) to Sir John French: *"Come aboard sir!"* An F. H. Townsend cartoon from *Punch*, 24 November 1915.

In November, 1915, Churchill was commissioned a Major in the Oxfordshire Yeomanry and in this photograph he is seen in the uniform of this regiment. He was transferred to the Grenadier Guards and later promoted Lieutenant-Colonel in the 6th Royal Scots Fusiliers.

F. E.: A True and Faithful Friend

Churchill first met Frederick Edwin Smith, later to become Earl of Birkenhead and one of Churchill's greatest friends, in the House of Commons in 1906. F. E., as he became known, was a brilliant orator, a legal genius, a Conservative MP, Solicitor-General, Lord Chancellor and Secretary of State for India. They were often political opponents. Clementine thought he was coarse, a drinker, a gambler and a bad influence on her husband, but he did become Randolph's godfather. Clementine did, however, like his wife Margaret (née Furneaux). On 18 December 1915 she wrote to Churchill following a visit made to her by F. E. There is no detail provided in the letter about what was said at their informal meeting, but Clemmie reasserts F. E.'s loyalty to Churchill, and his undaunted friendship. F. E. made a special visit to see Churchill in Flanders and give him advice. So too did Lord Curzon and Max Aitken.

Networking by Clementine

While he was away at war, Churchill asked Clementine to keep in touch with the British political masters on his behalf. Looking forward to his return to Parliament from the Western Front, he intended that he, along with several of his closest friends and colleagues (including Lloyd George, F. E., Bonar Law, Carson, Curzon and Lord Rothermere), form a new political association, an 'alternative government'. By entreating Clemmie to meet with them on a regular basis Churchill sought to ensure that upon his return the foundations of their nascent group were cemented.

Creature Comforts at the Front

Clementine sent food boxes from Fortnum and Mason: hot-water bottles, large towels, corned beef, Stilton cheese, sardines, ham, cream, dried fruits, steak pies, chocolate, potted meats, bottles of his 'old' brandy, peach brandy, port, whisky and cigars. Other requirements included a Corona typewriter (cost: 11 guineas), a volume of Robert Burns (so he could read passages to his Scottish soldiers), pairs of new riding breeches (from Tautz), khaki shirts, brown leather waistcoat, trench wading boots, a periscope, a sheepskin sleeping bag, a new Onoto pen, thick Jaeger drawers and vests, a sleeping cap and a new Glengarry cap.

Darling Clementine

Churchill took leave from the trenches on 2 March as the battalion came out of the line for a rest period. In London he spoke in the House of Commons and spent much time with F. E. Smith, Max Aitken, the Asquiths, Balfour, Sir Henry Dalziel, J. L. Garvin of *The Observer*, C. P Scott of *The Manchester Guardian* and, rather surprisingly, Lord Fisher, to whom Clementine said in effect, 'Keep your hands off my husband. You have all but ruined him once. Leave him alone now.' She did not enjoy his leave period and in a letter to him on the 25 March she wrote of her disappointment at how little time they spent together. Ominously, she warned their distance threatened to cool the ardour of their love and leave only a friendship in its place. Understandably, Churchill was alarmed at this development, and replied, in haste, reaffirming his devotion for her, and, no less, how vital she was to his happiness. Honest and fragile words.

In this group, taken in 1915, Churchill is standing beside General Emile Fayolle, Commander of the French Sixth and First Armies in the Battle of the Somme. In the following year, Churchill left the Army for good, since his command had disappeared with the amalgamation of the 6th Royal Scots Fusiliers with another battalion.

Three Best Things from Scotland

Churchill did not get his brigade. Sir John French had been recalled and Asquith regrettably blocked his promotion. Nevertheless on 5 January 1916 he arrived at Moolenacker near Meteren to take command of the 6th Battalion Royal Scots Fusiliers in General Furse's 19th Division. He brought with him his friend Archie (Sir Archibald) Sinclair (later 1st Viscount Thurso), two grooms, two black chargers, a huge pile of luggage including a long bath, and a boiler for heating water. His soldiers, who numbered 700 men, came from Ayrshire and Galloway, and he took pride in telling them that despite being an Englishman the three best things in his life had come from Scotland — his Dundee constituency, his regiment and Clemmie. His Royal Scots Fusiliers had suffered terribly in earlier fighting and the many new reserves and recruits needed encouragement. He was brilliant in his attitude. He organized a sports meeting (mule races, pillow fights, obstacle races), a concert in a big tent complete with raucous and joyful singing, and then a banquet in the evening, at which three cheers erupted for Churchill and one for Clemmie.

HMLS (His Majesty's Land Ship) *Centipede* was a remarkable invention and its creation well illustrates Winston Churchill's visionary ability. This photograph is of Mark IV, 1917.

HMS Centipede and the 'Devil's Coaches'

At the start of the war, Churchill had been urging the implementation of his armoured 'tractors' idea, and in early 1915, in a memorandum entitled 'Attack by Armour', he suggested to Field Marshal Sir Douglas Haig, commanding the British forces in France, that a prototype armoured caterpillar tractor be designed to cross over trenches and bomb, shell or mine craters. For various reasons prototypes and trials had come to naught. In February 1916 Churchill wrote to Clementine from the Front, recounting ecstatically how his 'caterpillar' had performed excellently in tests in front of Balfour, the First Lord of the Admiralty (and later Prime Minister). A year before, the Land Ships Committee of the Admiralty had been created, and while he was in power Churchill had ordered eighteen tracked 'landships' at a cost of £70,000. So Churchill's HMS *Centipede* was demonstrated to Lloyd George and Lord Kitchener — it worked — a hundred were ordered and the first British tanks went into action on 15 September 1916. The German defenders were horrified and called them the 'Devil's Coaches'.

Doing a Marlborough

Churchill praised the Royal Scots Fusiliers, who in the 100 days and nights of his command sustained 138 casualties. Churchill's HQ in a nuns' hospice was regularly shelled. In the field he was magnificent and utterly fearless; he personally led thirty-eight raids across no-man's-land to the enemy lines. Desmond Morton, a young Artillery major (later Churchill's Secret Service colleague), visited: 'I went over dead ground to Churchill's HQ. He had a sketching block in his hand, making a drawing of the enemy lines. He was "doing a Marlborough" calling up fire, demanding help on the flank and turning the whole thing into a major campaign rather than a trench raid to collar a few Germans.' Churchill was an excellent colonel. He insisted on the men taking care of their feet ('trench foot' was a major health problem); he led his troops when out of the line on route marches and insisted they sing. He inspected the trenches daily; making improvements, checking line telephones back to the artillery, making sure gas-mask drill was adhered to. He became immensely popular with men and officers. The blow fell when due to heavy casualties the 6th and 7th Battalions had to be amalgamated. Field Marshal Haig sent for him and told him to return to the House of Commons.

In March, 1916, Winston Churchill was back in England and in this photograph he is riding in Rotten Row, Hyde Park, with Clementine. The same month he appeared in the House of Commons to speak on the Navy Estimates and in his speech he was very critical of his successor and of the general sloth of British naval strategy.

The Bullet's Whistle

On his return from Flanders fields Churchill lost no time in making his voice heard in the House of Commons. On 23 May 1916, isolated on the Opposition benches, he spoke about the Western Front warfare: 'The trench population lives almost continuously under the fire of the enemy. It returns again and again, after being wounded twice and sometimes three times, to the front and to the trenches, and it is continually subject, without respite, to the hardest of tests that men have ever been called upon to bear, while all the time the non-trench population scarcely suffers at all, and has good food and good wages.' His service was with the Guards and Royal Scots Fusiliers — both infantry units — who suffered horribly. With the Scots Fusiliers was a draft of thirty-five men, twenty-six of whom had been wounded before, some of them severely, yet the bullet's whistle had never been heard by millions of men. His point (and he made it again a quarter of a century later) was that the administrative 'tail' of the British Army (who did none of the actual fighting) was far, far larger than the German Wehrmacht. But he was never successful, even when he was Prime Minister, in achieving a 'leaner' army.

Political Limbo: 'Winston is the Great Danger'

Back in London, Churchill took his place in the Commons as an MP, sitting isolated on the Opposition benches facing the Liberal-Conservative Coalition, and hoped and plotted for a return to Cabinet responsibility. In May 1916 he made two powerful speeches about aspects of Western Front soldiering. On 5 December five ministers resigned due to the appalling slaughter from July to December in the drawn-out Battle of the Somme. Asquith's downfall followed and Lloyd George became Prime Minister of the Second Coalition Parliament. The year of political limbo continued until Lloyd George offered Churchill the choice of Ministry for Air or of Munitions. The latter was a vital ministry with seventy departments and a staff of 12,000, employing two-and-a-half-million workers in the munitions and armament factories. Lord Derby, Secretary of State for War, wrote on 21 July 1917, four days after the new appointments, 'Lloyd George has made a "coup de main" when he appointed Winston Churchill and Edwin Montagu [who got India] ... Winston is the great danger because he will try to have a finger in the Admiralty and War Office pies. The appointment is very clever. He has removed from Asquith his two most powerful Lieutenants and provided for himself two first-class platform speakers.'

Brilliant Naval Inventions

In July 1917, just before becoming Minister of Munitions in Lloyd George's Government, Churchill produced a scheme for the capture of the two Frisian islands of Sylt and Borkum. He had always been fascinated by amphibious warfare. The object was to secure a base for naval forces and air squadrons who could tighten up the blockade of Germany and relieve the pressure of the U-boat war. His various plans deeply impressed the Prime Minister who had them specially printed for the War Cabinet and the Admiralty. One hundred bullet-proof lighters or torpedo-proof transports per division would carry the troops or marines to the island (of Borkum or Sylt); and there would be fifty tank-landing lighters fitted with wire-cutters in their bows. A shelving bow or drawbridge would allow the tanks to land under their own power and force a way through barbed-wire towards the enemy defences or forts. His second plan was to create an artificial island in the shallow waters of the Horn Reef north of the two islands. A number of flat-bottomed barges or caissons made of concrete would float when empty of water and be towed across to the site of the artificial island. On arrival seacocks would be opened, the barges would sink to the bottom and gradually fill with sand. Churchill specified their size: from 50 ft x 40 ft x 20 ft to 120 ft x 80 ft x 40 ft. They would become an artificial atoll, a torpedo — and weather-proof harbour with regular pens for RN destroyers and submarines. A year's preparation would be needed. Brilliant thinking — a man twenty-seven years ahead of the reality of Overlord in 1944.

With David Lloyd George in Whitehall, 1917. Lloyd George became Prime Minister on the resignation of Asquith. Asquith disliked Churchill and blamed him for the failure of the Gallipoli campaign. The final findings of the Committee of Investigation appeared soon after the fall of Asquith, but Lloyd George did not at first dare to include Churchill in his government.

Mr Winston Churchill (with eye on the Air Board): *"Any uniform suits me, thank you." Punch*, 13 June 1917.

In December 1916 the Asquith Government fell, and Lloyd George became Prime Minister. He wished to give Winston Churchill office in his new Government, but Bonar Law objected. At last, however, in July 1917, Lloyd George was able to offer Churchill a choice between the Air Ministry and the Ministry of Munitions. He chose the latter. It did not mean a seat in the Cabinet but, as he had been out of office for twenty months, it was the end of political exile.

'Great Republic of the West ... Coming to Our Aid'

Everything went wrong in 1917. The Russians collapsed on the Eastern Front, undermined by the Communist October Revolution. The Italians had been routed at Caporetto. The French Army had mutinied and their morale was badly damaged by the Verdun campaign and the failure of General Nivelle's offensive. In Britain hardly a family had escaped bereavement. U-boat sinkings had brought food rationing and price controls. There was universal conscription and Zeppelin raids and bloody stalemate at Passchendaele caused by barbed wire, mud, shell craters and deadly German machine-gun fire. Public morale was very low. In this grave situation Churchill spoke to the nation on 10 December. The Allied cause was in peril. Russia and France were *in extremis* and the British Empire — indeed civilization, faced an appalling future caused by overwhelming German power and intrigue backed by German gold and steel. But the United States, that 'Great Republic of the West', with its teeming millions, was now coming to the rescue.

German Generals Better

The disasters of 1917 were so terrible that Lloyd George favoured defensive operations on the Western Front until the American divisions would arrive

Churchill in somewhat unbecoming drainpipe trousers.

in strength. Churchill was convinced that there would be a heavy German offensive in 1918. Indeed there was and it nearly succeeded. Churchill pleaded for all possible manpower to bring the Army up to strength, even to the detriment of the Navy. He predicted the situation would be critical before June, and that any defeat on the Western Front would be fatal. Churchill felt that the Germans were fierce and formidable fighters and that their commanders were better. He was at the front on 21 March 1918 in Erich Ludendorff's 'All or Nothing' assault on the 50–mile line held by the British Army. After the collapse of Russia a million extra men and three thousand extra guns were deployed, mainly between Arras and St Quentin. Ludendorff's words were 'Wir müssen die Englander schlagen' — 'We must beat the British.' The battle lasted forty days and cost the British Army 300,000 casualties; in Churchill's eyes the world had never seen such an onslaught. Ludendorff had deployed sixty-six divisions and on 6 April, in a letter to Asquith, Churchill related how the Army had been perilously close to annihilation.

Ministry of Munitions

On assuming control of this sprawling empire in July 1917 Churchill concentrated the scattered departments of the Ministry of Munitions into ten large ones, each in the charge of a head who reported to him. He formed a council, comprising himself as chairman, the ten departmental chiefs and other key staff, which would meet daily. He was extremely busy visiting bases in France at the Hotel Ritz in Paris and the Chateau Verchocq near St-Omer, placed at his disposal by Lord Haig. In London, the Admiralty had commandeered the Hotel Metropole in Northumberland Street for him. Clementine was never sure where he was — in Paris assisting at Inter-Allied Councils, or sitting on the dais at Lille behind the Red Tabs [generals] or witnessing British troops recapturing Flemish cities. She observed the dissolution of two great empires, those of Germany and Russia, falling into ruin, and saw an opportunity for Churchill not only to present himself as an innovative and inventive military tactician, but also as someone ideally placed and capable of bringing together the faltering powers.

The Bolshevik Cradle: 'Treacherous Desertion'

After the Russian Bolsheviks signed the Treaty of Brest-Litovsk with the Germans in March 1918, there was a great danger that the two million tons of military stores and equipment, supplied by Britain, might fall into the hands of the Germans.

Consequently, British troops were sent to protect the vast dumps and depots at Murmansk, Archangel and Vladivostok. Then civil war broke out between Lenin's 'Reds' (Communists) and the 'White' (Tsarist) armies under Generals Deniken and his Cossacks, and Admiral Kolchak. With the Supreme Council for the Allies having consented to arms and money being sent, Churchill, in 1919 at the War Office, poured munitions and credits into anti-Bolshevik Russia to a value of nearly £73 million. He also raised and sent a force of 8,000 men, which secured the evacuation of the British garrisons. In April he made a speech: 'The miseries of the Russian people under the Bolshevists far surpass anything they suffered even under the Tsar.' He blamed Lenin and Trotsky for the Treaty: 'Every British soldier and French soldier killed last year [on the Western Front] was really done to death by Lenin and Trotsky, not in fair war, but by the treacherous desertion of an ally without parallel in the history of the world.' Both Deniken and Kolchak were defeated, and so General Ironside's Allied troops had to be withdrawn from Russia. Churchill admitted later that he had 'tried to strangle Bolshevism in its cradle'. Lloyd George said cynically that Churchill's 'ducal blood revolted against the wholesale liquidation of [Russian] Grand Dukes'.

A Day with the Tiger: a Grim Picture

On 28 March 1918, a week after Ludendorff's great offensive started, Lloyd George asked Churchill to spend a few days in France investigating the real position, in particular the apparent inactivity of the French Army. There was a possibility that General Pétain was regrouping the French Army around Paris and breaking off contact with the British forces. 'Go over and see everybody. Use my authority. See [Marshal] Foch, see Clemenceau [the seventy-six-year-old President, nicknamed 'the Tiger']. Find out for yourself whether they are making a really big move or not.' Accompanied by the Duke of Westminster, Churchill crossed the Channel on a destroyer and spent six days interviewing the key players, including Sir Douglas Haig, Foch, General Weygand and General Rawlinson. On 30 March he visited the front — vividly described in his *Thoughts and Adventures*. Near Moreuil he encountered the detritus of combat: injured horses, gore, munitions, wounded men — all conspiring to paint a grim picture of war. The old Tiger described the battle as 'un moment délicieux'. Well lobbied by Churchill, Lloyd George and Clemenceau, through their ambassadors in Washington, sent pressing messages to President Wilson urging that 120,000 American infantry be sent to Europe before the end of July. By the end of summer 1918 Ludendorff's advance was halted and the tide began to turn in the Allies' favour. The Armistice of 11 November ended the war, but the German hordes were undefeated and withdrew to the Rhine.

Field Marshal Paul Hindenburg, Kaiser Wilhelm II and General Erich Ludendorff pore over maps. After the war Ludendorff became a prominent nationalist leader, and a promoter of the betrayal concept, convinced that the German Army had been betrayed by Marxists and Republicans. He considered the Versailles Treaty to be an injustice and took part in the unsuccessful coups d'état of Wolfgang Kapp in 1920 and the Beer Hall Putsch of Adolf Hitler in 1923.

The Khaki and Coupon Election

Lloyd George's wartime Coalition Government went to the country on 28 December 1918. Five million voters turned out including many 'khaki' supporters who, in patriotic fervour, clamoured for vengeance, 'Hang the Kaiser', huge reparations, and for the party they hoped would give them an early release from the Armed Forces. Not only was it known as the 'Khaki Election' but also as the 'Coupon Election' as candidates supporting the Coalition were provided with coupons testifying to their loyalty. Unsurprisingly, the Coalition Party, which had been in power since 1915, supported by Lloyd George, Bonar Law and Churchill, romped home with 48 per cent of the total vote. Asquith himself was defeated. The Sinn Fein emerged with seventy-three members (who stayed away). Churchill had a rowdy campaign in Dundee but won comfortably.

At the end of hostilities 900,000 men were required for the Army of Occupation. These were selected out of the 3,500,000 men on the strength of the British Army. Churchill is here at the Grande Place in Lille in 1918, watching a march past of Allied troops before the problems of demobilization and occupation were settled.

The Empire's Great Deeds

Five weeks after the end of hostilities Churchill publicly thanked the loyal Dominions of the Commonwealth and Empire for mobilizing in defence of the 'Motherland' — without being summoned. He praised the formidable Canadians of the Vimy Ridge, the glorious Australians of Villers-Bretonneux, the dauntless New Zealanders of the Passchendaele crater fields, and the steadfast Indian Corps which held the line at Armentières.

Minister for Demobilization: Avoiding a Mutiny

As Secretary of State for War, Churchill visited and inspected the British Army troops in Cologne guarding the Rhine bridgeheads, infantry, armoured cars and tanks. The official plans for demobilization of most of the three-and-a-half-million troops under arms nearly caused a mutiny in the services. The so-called 'pivotal' men with skills in industry were scheduled to be released first, leaving the vast majority to wait. Men who had been several years in the line were not going to tolerate the newest recruits getting out of the services ahead of the old 'sweats' just because they had 'skills'. Troops on leave rioted and besieged the War Office, others on the Continent swarmed into Calais demanding shipment back to 'Blighty'. Churchill acted swiftly and sensibly, and ordered that first release would go to men with the longest service or with most wound-stripes. For a period of six months an average rate of 10,000 a day were discharged to civil life. In the meantime, the Army of Occupation in Germany needed 900,000 troops to garrison the British Zone. Churchill had formed sixty-nine 'Young Soldier' battalions of eighteen- and nineteen-year-olds who had been training in Britain when fighting ended. Experienced serving soldiers who stayed on received extra pay and bonuses. And three million were demobilized without further trouble.

After the Khaki Election in December, 1918, Churchill advanced further in the government hierarchy. He became War Minister and Air Secretary at once. Captain Wedgwood Benn, a persistent gadfly, mocked: "In his youth Winston was a medal-snatcher and self-advertiser; now he is a portfolio collector." Churchill gave one of his at once massive and subtle replies. Mr. Punch expressed it: 'The tank and the little brick. (Mr Churchill and Captain Wedgwood Benn) *"The tank, weighing thirty tons, is able to pass over a brick lying on the road without crushing it. This is a very important point."'* Mr Churchill. *Punch*, December 1918.

Churchill's Links with the Air Services: the Juggler

While at the Admiralty (1911-15), Churchill was responsible for the creation and development of the Royal Naval Air Service. From July 1917 to the end of the Great War he was at the huge Ministry of Munitions in charge of the design, manufacture and supply of all kinds of aircraft and air material needed for the war. From 1919-21 he was Air Minister as well as Secretary of State for War. His wife, however, disapproved, writing to him in March 1919 to suggest that he should resign from the Air Ministry and devote his whole attention to the War Office. Holding two offices, she said, required much juggling and he was, after all, a statesman not an entertainer. Playing on his self-esteem, she insisted that it would show strength of character if he were to give one up, and that he would be admired for doing so. She clearly believed that he was better off heading the War Office, quoting *The Observer* newspaper that there he was 'like a super Dreadnought manoeuvring about among pre-Dreadnoughts'.

Turbulent Life

The Churchills owned a charming small country house and farm at Lullenden, near East Grinstead. For several years from 1917 it was their second home (there was always a flat or house in London of course). On 12 September 1919, Clementine wrote wistfully to her husband, then in Paris, of how glad she was to be a source of peace and reassurance in his turbulent life. He, she told him, had been the best thing to have happened to her in her life; he had taken her from a boring, narrow existence and swept her into his colourful and exciting life, but, she felt, time was passing too quickly. It was their eleventh wedding anniversary.

Mobility of the Battlefield

Churchill was a modernizing influence in the post-war Army. From India to Russia, Egypt to Ireland, he claimed, armed forces the world over wanted armoured cars; mobile and manoeuvrable, these vehicles could move through villages or cross deserts with equal ease. And six months later in October 1919, he announced that he planned to replace at least half the cavalry with some very fast tank units — adding that he knew that the military experts would resist such a move with all their might. But he had served with the cavalry, fought in Flanders with the infantry and helped develop the tank. He was a military expert.

With Sir Henry Wilson on the Rhine. In 1919 Churchill became Secretary of State for War. In this photograph, he is on the Rhine, inspecting troops before their demobilization, in company with Sir Henry Wilson, Chief of the Imperial General Staff. Wilson did not altogether approve of Churchill's appointment and his comment in his diary was only one word—"Whew"!

Gallic Paranoia

The Duke of Westminster ('Bendor', Hugh Richard Arthur Grosvenor, the second Duke) had a large estate at Mimizan in Les Landes, south of Bordeaux. He and Churchill had been very close friends since the Boer War. Bendor had as many palatial homes as beautiful wives. In March 1920 Churchill went off to Mimizan to hunt boar and paint. One evening, M. André Lefèvre, the French Minister of War, poured out his grievances against England to Churchill. Britain, according to him, was worse than Germany in its treatment of France — but then, apparently, there wasn't a country in the whole world that had not in one way or another wronged or misjudged France. What clinched Churchill's opinion of him as a fool, however, was the derision with which he spoke of Clemenceau, whom Churchill knew and admired.

Emeralds for Clementine

In January 1921 came Churchill's only stroke of good fortune that year — a handsome legacy derived from the estate of Frances, wife of the 7th Duke of Marlborough, Churchill's great-grandmother, following the death in a railway accident of Lord Henry Vane-Tempest who had inherited initially. The Garron Tower Estates in County Antrim produced an income of £4,000 a year plus valuables such as emeralds (which went to Clementine) and other benefits. Churchill was able to finance most of the purchase of Chartwell with this legacy.

Blowing Bubbles

For the Churchills, 1921 was an appalling year. First of all Bill Hozier, Clementine's brother, to whom both were devoted, shot himself on 15 April in a Paris hotel room. Then Jennie, Lady Randolph, aged sixty-seven, fractured her ankle falling down a staircase in her London home. The leg was amputated, gangrene set in and she died on 29 June. Churchill wrote to Lord Curzon: 'The wine of life was in her veins. Sorrow and storms were conquered by her nature and on the whole, it was a life of sunshine.' Then, on 23 August, Clemmie's youngest, little Marigold, beloved 'Duckadilly', aged two years and nine months, died, probably of septicaemia, in her mother's arms. She had just learned to sing 'I'm For Ever Blowing Bubbles', her signature tune. Earlier that month, faithful Thomas Walden, manservant to Lord Randolph and then to Churchill, had died.

The Fortuneless Cat and Hungry Kittens

Churchill, under the pseudonym of Charles Morin, had exhibited a number of his oil paintings in the Parisian Galerie Druet, and six had been sold. Now *Strand Magazine* offered him £1,000 for two articles with pictures (mostly painted by Churchill) reproduced in colour. This pleased Churchill, who pointed out in a letter of February 1921 that his hobby was more than paying for itself. Clementine had her doubts about the magazine's offer, however, writing that while she shared her husband's keenness for the £1,000, she was worried that he would become the subject of trivial chit-chat and not be taken seriously, while the Colonies would consider that he was using up time better devoted to them. On the other hand, she was well aware that as she herself had no money, her husband needed every penny he could make to keep her and their children — his Cat and Kittens — fed, housed and clothed.

In January 1921 Churchill left the War Office and became Secretary of State for the Colonies. Cartoon from the *Daily Express*, 18 January 1921.

Churchill White Paper: the King Maker

In the early 1920s Churchill realized that there was a menace to the British Empire from the Bolsheviks, whom he saw as dangerous and seditious. He was, however, a realist. He kept South Africa and India in, but was lukewarm about Egypt. After the failure of Gallipoli, Australia and New Zealand were indeed rather distant. But he welcomed the Colonial Office in 1921 and found himself responsible for Palestine and Mesopotamia (modern Iraq). He created a Middle East Department, visited the Pyramids with Clementine, sketched and painted, and rode a camel for a photograph. The British, he stated, would run Iraq as they did some of the Indian states, under a figurehead ruler — King Feisal, in this instance. But Iraq was not a comfortable place to be and Churchill soon noted that he hated the country and wished the British had kept out of it. Elsewhere in the Middle East, the Emir Abdullah was entrusted with the government of Transjordania, and in June 1922 the Churchill White Paper was issued, committing the British Government to a Jewish national home in Palestine. Symbolically Churchill planted a tree beside the new Hebrew university on Mount Scopus.

A "futurist" landscape. Mr Churchill gets busy. *Punch*.

Mr Punch views Mr. Churchill's hobby of painting. A cartoon by Percey Fearon Poy for *Punch*.

To play down the importance of the 1921 Cairo conference, Churchill ostensibly enjoyed his favourite hobby, painting. This time he painted the Pyramids — while Lloyd George reshuffled his cabinet once more, in order to win stronger Conservative support.

Winston Churchill at Jerusalem, 28 March 1921, behind him T. E. Lawrence in conversation with Emir Abdullah.

Pictured at Government House, Jerusalem, 28 March 1921. Front row, from right to left: Clementine Churchill, Winston Churchill, Sir Herbert Samuel and Emir Abdullah of Transjordan.

Mr Winston Churchill (on his dahabeah): "Awfully rough on poor David in these trying times that I should have been 'taken away in the interest of the State.'" *Punch*. Everyone expected that Churchill would be asked to take the post of the Chancellor of the Exchequer, but the Tory leadership stubbornly declared that the interest of the State forbade Churchill's appointment to the second-in-rank. They feared that the Liberals would he too powerful in the coalition.

Troubles

Mr Gladstone in 1886 had commended the Home Rule Bill for Ireland, but it was rejected. In 1903 the Bill was destroyed by the House of Lords. Asquith tried again in April 1912. Two years later it was 'touch and go' — but the outbreak of war halted progress. By 1920, in spite of unceasing effort, Ireland had become ungovernable, except by violence, which, as Churchill wrote, was abhorrent to the British. He and Clementine had braved hostile crowds in Belfast. He had met Michael Collins and Arthur Griffith — the two Sinn Fein leaders — in his own home. Lloyd George and Churchill had always agreed that Ulster should remain part of the United Kingdom. A treaty providing self-government in a Free State for Southern Ireland (out of which Ulster was entitled to opt) was passed on 6 December 1921. On 7 January 1922 the Dublin Dáil Éireanns endorsed it by 64 votes to 57. Churchill had worked hard to broker this treaty. In April civil war broke out and dragged on until May 1923. Collins, who had tried so hard to implement the bill, was assassinated. A week later Arthur Griffith died of a heart attack. It seemed to Churchill that this left Britain with a depressing choice — to crush Ireland completely, or to give them what they wanted.

At the Irish Derby: *"Hang it all, Collins; she'll never do like this! She's got her legs crossed again!"*

The Colonial Secretary was a member of the Cabinet Committee dealing with the problem of Ireland. Fighting between the Sinn Fein Party and the British "Black and Tans" was fierce, and when Michael Collins and Arthur Griffiths came to London to sign the Treaty, which gave Ireland Dominion status, Winston Churchill worked tirelessly to help them establish a Provisional Government.

The Knock-a-bout Colonial

Clementine wrote her husband many forthright letters. From Beaulieu-sur-Mer on 18 February 1920 she lambasted the Canadian Hamar Greenwood, who became Irish Chief Secretary in 1920. Pleading for more justice in Ireland 'It makes me blush to think that men of the calibre of yourself and the P.M. should have listened to a man of the stamp of Hamar who is nothing but a blaspheming, hearty, vulgar, brave knock-a-bout Colonial ...'

Jingo, Extravagance and Fury

Mustapha Kemal Ataturk, hero of Gallipoli, ruler of Turkey, wished to repudiate the Sèvres Treaty of June 1920 which handed over to Britain and France all the non-Turkish territories — Arabia, Syria, Lebanon, Palestine and Mesopotamia. Greece was given Thrace, Smyrna, the Dodecanese and Rhodes. Armenia became independent. Kemal went to war with Greece and by mid-September 1922 had broken the Greek Armies. Smyrna was brutally sacked. The Turkish Army then moved north to threaten the neutral zone at the Dardanelles, of which the French and Italians as well as the British were guarantors. Lloyd George was very pro-Greek and Lord Curzon wrote, 'Lloyd George, Churchill and Birkenhead [F. E. Smith] excelled themselves in jingo, extravagance and fury.' Churchill drafted a belligerent press communiqué soliciting Dominion support in the event of a war with Turkey. The French and Italians ratted and it was left to General Charles Harington in charge of the small British force in Chanak, a small township overlooking the Dardanelles, to negotiate with Kemal. He later signed an armistice convention which restored Eastern Thrace to Turkey. A revolution took place in Athens, King Constantine was expelled and Lloyd George resigned, Bonar Law taking his place. To Churchill the return of the Turks to Europe meant nothing but trouble.

The Peace Maker

A daughter, Mary, was born to Clementine on 15 September 1922. A month later Churchill suffered acute appendicitis in the midst of a General Election. He was still MP for Dundee, won in 1918 with a majority of over 15,000. Clementine, with a seven-week-old baby, set out on 6 November for Scotland to rally Churchill's supporters. She addressed countless meetings in packed rowdy halls, wearing a string of pearls (but probably not the emeralds), and was heckled and spat upon by women. Their friend General Edward Spears reported back to her husband: 'Clemmie's bearing was magnificent — like an aristocrat going to the guillotine in a tumbril.' The invalid had been made a Companion of Honour in the Resignation Honours list. Clementine told the meetings of Churchill's settlement of the Irish question and of his giving the Boers self-government. But in the public eye he was seen as a 'warmonger'. She wrote to her husband that she was presenting him as a sweet, cherubic peacemaker. On 11 November, he arrived in Dundee, very weak, talked sitting down and lost his seat by 10,000 votes. The family, defeated and dejected, let their house at 2 Sussex Square and fled to the Villa Rêve d'Or (Golden Dream) in Cannes. Clementine played tennis. Churchill continued writing *The World Crisis*, gambled modestly and painted gloriously in the Riviera sunshine.

The Prince of Wales's Toe

During the winters of 1921 and 1922 Churchill saw a fair amount of the 'P of W' [Prince of Wales, future King Edward VIII]. Clementine was much away, grieving for her family losses and later nursing her fifth pregnancy. Churchill danced the light fantastic at the houses of the Laverys [his painting gurus], the Sassoons [a millionaire art collector and family] and the Rutlands [Duke and Duchess]. One night, Churchill trod with his heel upon the Prince of Wales's toe — the Prince, although he gave a cry of pain, did not complain.

Winston Churchill as paternal adviser to the Prince of Wales.

A group photograph taken at 10 Downing Street on the occasion of a luncheon given in 1922 to M. Raymond Poincaré, French Prime Minister from 1922 till 1924. Sitting in the front row, left to right: Winston Churchill, Earl Balfour, Raymond Poincaré, David Lloyd George and Marshal Philippe Pétain.

Purchase of Chartwell

Churchill fell in love with a large manor house — Chartwell — near Westerham and only twenty-four miles from Westminster. An Elizabethan house with Victorian additions set in eighty acres; it was somewhat dilapidated and needed much expensive work and architect's fees to restore it. Greatly helped by his recent inheritance, Churchill paid £5,000 for it without telling Clementine. At the wheel of his ancient Wolseley car, he drove his three children, Randolph, Diana and Sarah, to view the property. It was gaunt and long-abandoned, with ivy, weeds, nettles, laurel, firs and rhododendrons clustered around it. The children were excited by the inspection and asked him to buy it. He already had! His mind was fixed on plans for landscaping the park and lakes. Clementine hated the purple and mauve rhododendrons and was dismayed by the rundown state of the property.

Flying Cloud and 'The Office'

The kittens and Clementine spent the autumn of 1923 in Hosey Rigge ('Rosy Pigge' to the family), a charming rented house on the Common above Westerham. Chartwell was close by and was being expensively and extensively renovated. The Duke of Westminster (Bendor, or Benny) owned a large four-master yacht, the *Flying Cloud*, which could sail at 12 knots and accommodate sixteen guests. Leaving Clementine with a sore throat and her children at Rosy Pigge, Churchill joined the Westminsters on this magnificent boat. Churchill was happy to write to his wife regaling her with details of his luxurious holiday — the weather perfect, his host and hostess delightful; he painted when he wanted or went ashore to enjoy a game of polo, while at night there was the casino (the office) ...

Winston re-ratted and returned to the Tory fold. Here he and Clementine are campaigning for the seat of Epping Forest in the General Election of 29 October 1924.

Re-ratting

Out of office, with no seat, 1923 was a year of limbo for Churchill. Clementine counselled him to remain on good terms with the 'old' liberals as they might eventually take him back.

Rusholme, in Greater Manchester, was one of several seats that Churchill considered. He had a meeting, in mid-August, with the Conservative Prime Minister, Stanley Baldwin (in succession to Bonar Law who, seriously ill, resigned on 22 May). However, another election took place on 6 December and the next month Ramsay MacDonald became the first Labour Prime Minister, supported by Asquith and the Liberals. Churchill was now veering strongly towards rejoining the Conservatives. The Labour Government was defeated that October and, after barely ten months, another general election was called. Churchill was returned for the Conservative seat of Epping, making his famous comment: 'Anyone can rat,' he commented, 'but it takes a certain amount of ingenuity to re-rat.' To his surprise Baldwin invited him to become Chancellor of the Exchequer. The Conservative Party was flabbergasted. He had 'crossed the floor' for a second time and once again was in the Conservative fold. The Churchills moved into No. 11 Downing Street in January 1925.

The Churchill family off to the House of Commons to hear his budget speech. From left to right, Diana, Randolph, Winston and Clementine. The other two daughters, Sarah and Mary were too young to go.

Days of Labour

The cost of renovating Chartwell had risen to £17,648 by the end of 1924. Clementine had taken great interest in its progress (or lack of it). The new room ceilings fell down twice and destroyed expensive chandeliers. The old building was gradually transformed into a tall house in mellow red brick. Built on a steep slope, the rooms had different levels — a hall, five reception rooms, nineteen bedrooms and dressing rooms, eight bathrooms, domestic offices, stables, three garages, a large studio and three cottages. On 17 April 1924 Churchill moved in with two vanloads of clothes and furniture, and an entourage that included his children, Lily the kitchen maid, Aley the chauffeur and Sergeant Thompson the detective. Clementine was in Dieppe visiting her mother. He wrote to her describing how hard they were all working on the house and garden, with the help of two gardeners and six workmen. In the evenings, after labouring all day, they would have a bath, and then play the gramophone and mah-jongg. Churchill himself drank champagne at every meal, and watered-down claret in between. Only Clementine, he wrote, was missing.

The Chancellor and the Gold Standard

Churchill's first important task as Chancellor of the Exchequer was to visit Paris to renegotiate the international agreements on War Debt and post-war reparations. He reported fighting hard with the Americans, even over trifling amounts such as £100,000. Next came a return by the United Kingdom to the Gold Standard, suspended during the war. The Weimar Republic German mark had collapsed; the French franc had lost three-quarters of its value. The Treasury advocated a return; a select committee of economists recommended a return. J. M. Keynes predicted disaster. Churchill went ahead with grave doubts, and a return to the Gold Standard was included in his 28 April Budget. The pound was revalued upwards and British exports suffered dramatically. Keynes was right. The other experts were wrong. The coal-mining industry employed a million men and the higher pound acutely damaged their exports. A subvention of £19 million to the miners postponed strikes until May 1926.

Churchill's Forecast of Atomic and Flying Bombs

In 1925 Churchill penned a note of how technical inventions would shape future war. 'May there not be methods of using explosive energy incomparably more intense than anything heretofore discovered? Might not a bomb no bigger than an orange be found to possess a secret power to destroy a whole block of buildings — nay, to concentrate the force of a thousand tons of cordite and blast a township at a stroke? Could not explosives even of the existing type be guided automatically in flying machines by wireless or other rays without a human pilot, in ceaseless procession upon a hostile city, arsenal, camp or dockyard?' The shape of things to come — a nuclear bomb and (Hitler's) flying bombs.

Tea with Mussolini

After her mother died in Dieppe, Clementine and Goonie (Jack Churchill's wife) spent two weeks in Rome, staying at the Embassy. Mussolini, leader of the Italian Fascist Government, came to tea and, Clementine wrote to her husband, was charming. She was much taken by his manners and his eyes, and noted that he loved music and played the violin. She also remarked that everyone treated him with deference, as though he were a king, and that his followers were fanatically devoted to him. Moreover, Il Duce sent her a beautiful signed photograph 'A la Signora Winston Churchill, Devotamente, B Mussolini'. The photograph was prominently displayed in Chartwell Manor until the outbreak of the Second World War.

"*Pull Philip, pull David.*" *Punch* cartoon. The Gold Standard had not been Churchill's idea, nevertheless, the measure aroused irate opposition against the Chancellor, with Lloyd George and Philip Snowden as chief noisemakers. Each proposed amendments contrary to those of his fellow critic.

Daily Express cartoon, 13 February 1925. There was speculation as to whether the price of tobacco would rise in the coming Budget. Cigarettes were eleven-pence for twenty at this time.

The Children at Chartwell

When either Churchill or Clementine was away from home, and the other looked after the children, their letters were always full of news about their youngsters. For example, while Clementine was in Rome, Churchill wrote to her from Chartwell about what a pleasure it was to have them, how sweet they were, and that he could not decide which he loved the most. Mary, aged three, breakfasted with him; Sarah, aged eleven, dined with him; and Diana, aged sixteen, talked politics with him, with some intelligence and knowledge. He added that she was growing up and would soon be making her mark on their lives.

Cat Burglar and Marauder

As Chancellor of the Exchequer Churchill spoke in the House of Commons on 22 April 1926 of the debates before and after his second Budget. An analysis was made of the epithets he received.

The word 'robbery' or 'robbed' was used sixty-seven times; 'mean' fifteen; 'raid' eleven; 'confiscation' and 'plunder' each ten; 'breach of faith' nineteen; and then

A David Low cartoon from the *Star*, 11 February 1926. Mr Baldwin on himself: *"The life of a shop girl and that of a Prime Minister are very similar.... The only difference is that she has to give people what they want; I have to say that they can't have it."*

'theft', 'filch', 'grab', 'betrayal', 'outrage', 'infamy', 'rascality', 'perfidy', 'paltry', 'shabby', 'despicable' and 'dastardly'. Churchill did receive some compliments: 'the villain of the piece', 'robber', 'marauder', 'cat burglar' and 'Artful Dodger'.

'He Thinks He is Napoleon'

The General Strike lasted for eight days in May 1926. The Trades Union Congress and the Labour Party guaranteed the striking miners their full support even if this became a General Strike. The mine owners and the miners rejected the Samuel Commission. When Churchill's subsidy to the miners ended on 30 April, Ernest Bevin, the TUC leader, called a strike of vital services. Transport closed down, iron and steel trades, building, electricity and gas-power plants came to a standstill. The Government called for volunteers to act as special police and bus and engine drivers. Churchill produced the *British Gazette* on the printing presses of the *Morning Post*. The Royal Navy operated the presses, London University printing students set the newspaper type and the Automobile Association provided couriers to distribute the papers. Irish guards protected the *British Gazette* staff; the paper had a record circulation of 2.2 million. Baldwin removed himself to Aix-les-Bains for three and a half weeks and left Churchill in charge to deal with the continuing coal strike.

J. C. C. Davidson, Parliamentary Secretary to the Admiralty, wrote to Baldwin: 'He [Churchill] thinks he is Napoleon.'

Only Four Cigars a Day

Chartwell was proving very expensive to run. Churchill proposed renting it and taking the family to live 'cheaply' and pleasantly in Dinard, Brittany. Then in late summer 1926 he drafted a memorandum, presumably for a readership of two, inflicting severe savings. The Red Poll cattle, chickens, ponies (except Diana's) including Energy, his last polo pony, pigs — all would be sold. The staff would be decimated: Christmas holidays in Downing Street; only picnics with hampers at Chartwell; every bill was to be shown to Churchill, who was also going to inspect the Wine Book weekly; no champagne was to be bought, no port to be opened. He limited cigars to four a day (scarcely a hardship to the rest of the family) and not for guests — they would be offered only cigarettes. Meals were to be reduced to just one course for lunch and two courses and pudding for dinner. No cream was to be bought, nor fruit nor fish. Laundry, too, would be controlled — for instance, Churchill felt that he could get by adequately on two white shirts a week.

The winter of 1926 was spent in London, then life resumed as before. In 1925 Churchill spent £259 on coal and fuel at Chartwell and £275 on cars. In 1926 he spent £309 on wines and spirits and £163 on cigars. In the early 1930s he gave Clementine on the first of each month £300 for housekeeping. For a rough modern equivalent multiply those figures by thirty or forty. He hoped to budget Chartwell on £250 per month.

The World Crisis and Other Books

The five-volume *History of the First World War* started to appear from 1923 onwards. The advance for each volume was about £2,500 and royalties were high. *The Times* paid £5,000 for serial rights. Each book was about 450 pages long and produced by Thornton Butterworth. In New York Charles Scribner produced each volume, often with a different title, and eventually Churchill's American sales yielded vast royalties. His *My Early Life*, published in 1930, sold 11,200 copies in England and 6,600 in America. It was translated into thirteen languages and eventually a film script was sold.

His *Life of Marlborough* earned a £10,000 advance from George Harrap, plus £5,000 from Scribner's and another £5,000 for serial rights to *The Daily Telegraph*. These were huge earnings for a very successful author.

Winston Churchill with
his son Randolph during a
holiday in Italy, *c.* 1924.

India: Hindus and Muslims

Churchill as a young soldier had had years of experience in India. By 1931, he
was firmly convinced that the removal of British power there would lead not
only to large-scale violence and bloodshed between Muslims and Hindus, but
also to the end of the British Empire. He commented that while both religions
contained so many clever and delightful people, they would never be able to get
on together, the rift between them was insurmountable. Sadly, he was seen to
have been right when partition took place some seventeen years later: millions
lost their lives and the 'Jewel in the Crown' was no more.

Accident and Convalescence in New York

In December 1931 Churchill was nearly killed by a car on Fifth Avenue between
76th and 77th Streets, on his visit with Clementine and daughter Sarah on a
lucrative forty-lecture tour. He had a severe scalp wound, two cracked ribs

and was generally much bruised. His doctor, Otto C. Pickhardt, wrote a letter: 'This is to certify that the post-accident convalescence of Hon. Winston S. Churchill <u>necessitates</u> the use of alcoholic spirits especially at meal times. The quantity is naturally indefinite but the minimum requirements would be 250 cubic centimeters' [about a third of a bottle]. This was at a time when America was in the grip of Prohibition.

Churchill remained bed-bound in the Lennox Hill Hospital for eight days, then convalesced at the Waldorf-Astoria Hotel and finally went to recover in Nassau, West Indies.

The Meeting with Adolf Hitler

In the autumn of 1932 Winston and son Randolph with the 'pasha's' entourage were in south Germany. The inspection of the Blenheim battlefield was the main objective for his book on Marlborough. Father and son then spent a week in Munich staying at the Regina Hotel. There, by chance, they met Ernst 'Putzi' Hanfstängl, a local art publisher who was a friend of Hitler's. Putzi was a gregarious part-American character who sang and danced and played the piano (including many contemporary English tunes) and persuaded Churchill that he should meet Hitler who visited the hotel every afternoon. Churchill agreed as he had no national prejudices against Hitler at that time, and did not know his character, record or doctrine.

Hanfstängl went up to Hitler's room, where he told the Führer: 'Don't you realize the Churchills are sitting in the restaurant? ... They are expecting you and will think this a deliberate insult.' Hitler said that he was unshaven and had too much to do. Hanfstängl suggested he shave and come down anyway, and went back to the party. But Hitler never showed up.

Hanfstaengl was one of Hitler's most intimate followers. For much of the 1920s, he introduced Hitler to Munich's high society and helped polish his image. Hanfstaengl fell completely out of Hitler's favour after he was denounced by Unity Mitford and moved to England. In 1942 he was sent to the USA.

Churchill's poor health forced him to give up sports. He replaced them with bricklaying. But the bricklayers protested against a non-union member working at Chartwell Manor. Churchill filled out a card for the bricklayer's union and applied for membership. He did a considerable amount of building on his own grounds and was an accomplished bricklayer. He was essentially an open-air man with strong and capable hands. The photograph below, taken in 1928, shows him assisted by his daughter, Sarah, hard at work building the wall at Chartwell.

Chartwell: Churchill's 'Farm'

The initiative, daring and vision of the redevelopment of Chartwell Manor were Churchill's. He was the mastermind. He constructed (often literally) an intricate system of lakes, dams and waterworks filled with waterfowl, cranes, swans and fish. He had a tennis court laid out (Clementine was a good player).

He built cottages and garden walls and installed an open-air, heated, filtered and floodlit swimming pool. He planted three hundred asparagus plants; plum, apple and pear trees; strawberries and every fruit that could grow in Kent. It was his farm, and he was determined it would pay whatever it might cost him. It did of course cost. To run the estate efficiently Churchill was helped by nine indoor servants, two secretaries, a chauffeur, three gardeners, a groom for horses and ponies, a working bailiff and a nanny or governess for his four young children. At one stage — hard-pressed by poor investments — in the spring of 1938 he put Chartwell Manor up for sale at £20,000 (less than he had spent on it). Fortunately an Anglo-South African financier, Sir Henry Strakosch, came to his rescue.

Randolph and Diana with their father at Chartwell, late 1920s.

Winston Churchill at home in his little Foreign Office.

'Little Foreign Office'

In the 'wilderness years' of the 1930s (the Government having fallen in the May 1929 elections), Chartwell was Churchill's fortress. In effect he formed his own intelligence service, greatly helped by his two friends, the German-speaking Professor Lindemann and Desmond Morton. The former, a physicist, and aerodynamics and statistics expert, provided information about many aspects of German military progress. The latter, Director of the Industrial Intelligence Centre under the Cabinet Office, was allowed by the Prime Minister, Ramsay MacDonald, to keep Churchill fully informed of foreign affairs. From Chartwell direct telephone lines to the Central Telegraph agency (at a cost of £4,500) provided Churchill's 'Little Foreign Office', as it was christened, with efficient and rapid communications with the outside world.

Invaders

The BBC had a monopoly of the airwaves in the mid-1930s. Their policy was heavily biased (as was the Government) towards appeasement with the European dictators. Rather surprisingly Churchill was allowed to make a radio broadcast to the nation on 16 November 1934, In it he pointed out that England had not been invaded for nearly a thousand years, protected as the country was by the sea and the Royal Navy. Now, though, there were aeroplanes — it would take bombers only a few hours to reach Britain from Central Europe, and the Navy had no defence against air attack.

The German U-Boat Threat: 'Swimming in a Halcyon Sea'

Churchill noted, in May 1935, that Germany was increasing its army from twenty-two to thirty-six divisions as fast as it could. Its navy was building powerful battle cruisers and had started a U-boat development. He recalled how comparatively easy it was to manufacture these vessels — and how quickly it could be done: 'I remember in November 1914 arranging for Mr Schwab, of Bethlehem [Steel in the USA], to make twenty submarines in ... the incredibly short period of six months.' The vessels were made in the USA in sections, shipped by rail to Canada for reasons of neutrality and welded together. Churchill knew how devastating the U-boat warfare had been in 1917. British shipping losses had been appalling. He tried to persuade the House of Commons of the dangers that lay ahead. He described the Government policy of appeasement as 'swimming in a halcyon sea, nothing but balmy breezes ... and calm weather.' He also noted that Germany was led by a 'handful of triumphant desperadoes'.

Winston Churchill keeping himself occupied during the 'Wilderness Years'.

Building work at Chartwell was therapeutic to Winston Churchill during the mid-1930s.

Thank God for the French Army

Churchill made a speech in the Théâtre des Ambassadeurs in Paris on 24 September 1936, in which he divided the world into three types of nation — that governed by the Nazis, that governed by Bolshevism, and that which governed itself. Britain and France belonged to the last category and now he called for them to stand together in the face of aggression from the others.

Four years before speaking in the House of Commons, Churchill had thanked God for the French Army. Now, in 1936, he reiterated this sentiment, adding that it was the best army in the world. Four years later it crumbled and fell to pieces.

The King's Abdication

Wallis Simpson, the hard, beautiful, twice-divorced American socialite was King Edward VIII's mistress. Churchill had known the King from his youth and was devoted to him. He tried all he could to avoid an abdication as the King was determined to marry her, proposing the idea of a morganatic marriage in which Mrs Simpson would have remained a private citizen and any children would not have been heirs to the throne. The Cabinet rejected the idea; the Commonwealth would have hated it. Clementine disagreed with her husband completely. Churchill then suggested that Mrs Simpson could become Duchess of Cornwall in a morganatic marriage. The Abdication eventually took place on 11 December 1936. Churchill was deeply moved and upset.

Churchill, the Hated Enemy

Adolf Hitler hated Winston Churchill. His diatribes started in the 1930s. On 9 October 1938, the Führer wrote: 'We are today a people of power and strength such as Germany has never known before. However, experience must strengthen our resolution to be careful and never omit anything that should be done to protect the Reich. We have, on the other side, statesmen who we believe, also want peace ... If Churchill came to power in Great Britain instead of Chamberlain we know it would be the aim to unleash immediately a world war against Germany. He makes no secret of it.'

Incomprehensible French

Churchill was a frequent visitor to Paris and usually combined politics, military planning and socializing in equal amounts. Sir Eric Phipps, the British Ambassador, wrote in 1938, 'Winston Churchill's stay here has continued in an increasingly kaleidoscopic manner. Almost every facet of French political life has been presented to him at and between meals [leading French statesmen Édouard Herriot, Paul Reynaud, Léon Blum, Joseph Paul-Boncour, Édouard Daladier, Alexis Saint-Léger Léger, Pierre-Étienne Flandin, Georges Mandel and Louis Marin; and General Maurice-Gustave Gamelin, plus a clutch of French journalists]. He wanted to see a Communist, but I strongly advised against this, and he abstained ... His French is most strange and at times incomprehensible.' A few months later, in July, Churchill and Clementine were present at the State visit to France of King George VI and Queen Elizabeth. On that occasion Churchill wrote articles for *The Daily Telegraph* about the culture and the sights of France — an idyllic stay in a free country.

'The Prof': Frederick Alexander Lindemann

Son of an Alsatian father and an American mother, educated in England and Germany, this extraordinary man became not only a close friend of the Churchills but Churchill's *éminence grise*. A bachelor, teetotaller, rich, a vegetarian with strong prejudices about colour and race, in many ways he was the exact opposite of Churchill. Professor Lindemann ('the Prof') presided over the Clarendon Laboratory, was Professor of Experimental Philosophy at Oxford, an expert in physics, a skilled pilot and during the 1930s became indispensable to Churchill. With his slide-rule he was able to explain complex technologies and scientific data in terms that a layman could understand. Violently anti-German, he was particularly knowledgeable on air warfare and able to explain complex matters such as radar in layman's terms. He was a trusted friend who, like Churchill, had seen the storm clouds rolling over the horizon and had joined him in trying to warn the Government of approaching disaster. This, along with the fact that he could decipher signals sent from afar and explain them in clear everyday terms, was in Churchill's eyes sufficient to qualify him for the role as the Prime Minister's closest adviser during the war. Later, General 'Pug' Ismay, Chief of Staff to the Prime Minister, wrote: 'Churchill used to say that the Prof's brain was a beautiful piece of mechanism, and the Prof did not dissent from that judgement.' Lindemann later became Lord Cherwell.

Churchill's Toy Shop

Military Intelligence Research (MIR) was set up in 1939 and soon became MD1 (Military Defence 1). It was a secret establishment in Whitchurch near Aylesbury (and Chequers) with a staff of 250, devising cheap, effective and nasty weapons (twenty-six in all). These ranged from booby traps, sticky bombs, limpet mines, fluvial mines, to a W bomb, a castrator and other nasties! Millis Jefferis and Norman Macrae were the two experts in creating mayhem. The jealous War Office departments were furious, because 'Churchill's Toy Shop' was run independently, with 'the Prof' as the intelligent anti-Nazi 'go-between' between this highly secret organization and Churchill.

Max Aitken: 'Tammany Hall Boss'

Clementine disliked this millionaire Canadian gnome who later, as Lord Beaverbrook, became a major newspaper proprietor and Unionist MP. He also held important government posts under Lloyd George and Churchill. From 1916 he became firm friends with Churchill. Once, Clementine described him as a good foul-weather friend; Churchill called him a 'Tammany Hall Boss' while the 'Beaver' informed Churchill that there was in him 'the stuff of which tyrants are made.' After the Second World War he frequently lent his Riviera house at Cap d'Ail to the Churchills. Charles Moran, Churchill's doctor, described Max: 'The people he gathers round him at Cherkley are not interested in books. Their conversation is earthy and full of the frailty of man.'

The Munich Agreement: 'All is Over'

Neville Chamberlain tried his best to avert the threatening war clouds. In September 1938 he flew to parley with Hitler and on the 29th he went to Munich where he met Hitler, Mussolini and the French Prime Minister, Édouard Daladier. On 10 October he returned brandishing the notorious piece of paper, and promising 'Peace for our time'. It seemed to promise that Germany and Britain would never again go to war. Four days later in the House of Commons Churchill declared, 'All is over. Silent, mournful, abandoned, broken Czechoslovakia recedes into the darkness.' The fleet was mobilized. Trenches were dug in the London parks as protection from air raids. Sirens were tested and gas masks distributed. Churchill wrote trenchant fortnightly articles in *The Daily Telegraph* and toiled at Chartwell at his *History of the English Speaking Peoples*. He wrote to Clementine, who was in the West Indies on the yacht *Rosaura* belonging to their friend Lord Moyne (Walter Edward Guinness, 1st Baron Moyne), saying that he did not think war was imminent for Britain. In March 1939 Hitler, ignoring the Munich Agreement, invaded Czechoslovakia; in April Mussolini sent his Fascist armies into Albania.

Neville Chamberlain meets Hitler at Munich, 15 September 1938. With them are British Ambassador Sir Neville Henderson and German Foreign Minister Joachim Ribbentrop.

The Path to War

Churchill made another stirring broadcast to the USA from London on 8 August 1939, conjuring up the image of millions of German and Italian soldiers, supposedly on manoeuvre, preparing against the day when such dangerous peoples as the Dutch, the Albanians, the Jews should suddenly attack them and wrest from them their lebensraum ...

At dawn on 1 September Hitler unleashed his Storm Troopers, the Wehrmacht and the deadly Stukas of the Luftwaffe on Poland. The next day France and Britain issued an ultimatum demanding Germany's withdrawal and respect for Polish sovereignty. At 11.15 on 3 September Neville Chamberlain in his sad, defeated, melancholy voice announced that the ultimatum had expired and, consequently, Britain was at war with Germany.

Friday 1 September 1939.

11.15 a.m. Sunday 3 September 1939: "*I am speaking to you from the Cabinet Room at 10 Downing Street. This morning the British Ambassador in Berlin handed the German Government a final Note stating that, unless we heard from them by 11 o'clock that they were prepared at once to withdraw their troops from Poland, a state of war would exist between us. I have to tell you now that no such undertaking has been received, and that consequently this country is at war with Germany.*"

'Winston is Back'

From November 1911 to 1915 Churchill was First Lord of the Admiralty and made a significant impact on the traditional Admirals and their Dreadnoughts. When on 5 September 1939 — at the outbreak of the Second World War — Churchill was given charge of the Admiralty for the second time, the message was sent out immediately to the Navy afloat and to shore establishments: 'Winston is back.'

Russia: 'a Riddle, Wrapped in a Mystery, Inside an Enigma'

Hitler and Stalin signed a Nazi-Soviet Pact in August 1939 and then jointly overran Poland despite the heroic defence of Warsaw and the bravery of the Polish defenders. Russia warned Hitler off making incursions into the East, but as Churchill commented in a broadcast on 1 October, you couldn't tell what Russia, that enigmatic, mysterious nation, would do. 'I cannot forecast to you the action of Russia. It is a riddle, wrapped in a mystery, inside an enigma ... Russia has warned Hitler off his Eastern dreams.'

"All is forgiven: Welcome Home" Tribune 20 October 1939. When war started Neville Chamberlain was forced to invite Winston Churchill, Anthony Eden and Duff Cooper to rejoin the Conservative Government, Churchill becoming again First Lord of the Admiralty, the position he had held at the commencement of the First World War.

Signature of 'Naval Person'

On 11 September 1939 President Roosevelt wrote to Churchill. They had only met once in the Great War at a dinner at Gray's Inn and 'I had been struck by his magnificent presence in all his youth and strength'. Roosevelt wrote: 'Because you and I occupied similar positions in the World War I want you to know how glad I am that you are back again in the Admiralty ... What I want you and the Prime Minister [Chamberlain] to know is that I shall at all times welcome it if you will keep me in touch personally with anything you want me to know about. You can always send sealed letters through your [diplomatic] pouch or my pouch'. Churchill replied promptly, using his famous alias 'Naval Person' — the start of almost one thousand communications each spread over the next five years, until the President's death.

The First Lord gave a timely warning. In the first of his stirring wartime speeches, delivered on 1 October 1939, he declared: "It was for Hitler to say when the war would begin. But it is not for him, or his successors, to say when it will end."

Untrustworthy and Unstable

John (Jock) Colville joined the Foreign Office in September 1939 and over a period of time became head of Churchill's Private Office and a loyal friend of both the Churchills. On 1 October he listened to Churchill's inspiring radio speech. 'He certainly gives one confidence and will, I suspect, be Prime Minister before this war is over. Nevertheless, judging from his record of untrustworthiness and instability, he may, in that case, lead us into the most dangerous paths. But he is the only man in the country who commands anything like universal respect, and perhaps with age he has become less inclined to undertake rash adventures.' Colville kept a brilliant diary from 1938 until 1966.

Plan Catherine

On his arrival at the Admiralty at the end of 1939 Churchill devised the extraordinary 'Plan Catherine' (after Catherine the Great of Russia). A fleet would support two or three capital ships of the Royal Sovereign class into the Baltic to protect Scandinavia from German attack and to deny supplies of Narvik-Lulea iron ore (vital to the German armaments industry) and certain food supplies. The fleet would comprise five cruisers, two flotillas of destroyers plus submarines and a fleet repair ship. Bearing in mind the naval fiasco at the Dardanelles, a dozen special minesweepers with caissons or super-blisters would deal with enemy minefields. Catherine would sail into action in March 1940 when the ice floes and bergs had melted. But because of the devastating use of German air power, Catherine was abandoned in January 1940.

The Phoney War (US)/The Bore War (UK)

For nearly eight months the German and French Armies looked at each other from the Siegfried and Maginot lines on the northern borders of France. Hitler was terrifying and subdued the brave Poles with Stalin's very active connivance. The British Army and the RAF were far too small to tackle the enemy offensively. The French could and perhaps should have acted more aggressively. It was called the 'Phoney War' particularly in the North American media and the 'Bore War' in England. The Navy was immediately in action. The German U-boat fleet was very active and inflicted huge shipping losses: in the first fortnight of the war they sank 110,000 tons of British merchant ships and, indiscriminately, many Finnish, Dutch, Norwegian, Swedish, Greek and Belgian ships. But a considerable number of German ships were captured. On 3 September 1939 the passenger liner SS *Athenia*, carrying some

Captain Hans Langdorff scuttles the *Graf Spee*, 17 December 1939. A success after months of frustration was welcome news at home.

On 23 February, 1940, the crews of the cruisers *Ajax* and *Exeter*, which gained fame in the *Graf Spee* action, marched through the City of London to Guildhall, where they were entertained to lunch. Winston Churchill and Neville Chamberlain watched the march go past.

1,100 passengers, including over 300 Americans, was sunk with huge losses. Goebbels, Hitler's PR spokesman, declared that Churchill had done it to induce America to come into the war. It was in fact sunk by the German U-boat, *U-30*, probably mistaken for an armed cruiser. The Royal Navy lost the *Courageous*, *Royal Oak* and the *Rawalpindi*, but the German pocket battleship *Graf Spee* was cornered by three British cruisers and forced to scuttle itself. And the Royal Navy rescued hundreds of captured British sailors from the *Almark* in a Norwegian fjord. In April 1940 Hitler invaded Norway and the Royal Navy had many gallant actions but after a few weeks the small British land force was evacuated. Chamberlain was forced to resign, partly as a result of the Norwegian fiasco, but also because Hitler sent his Luftwaffe and Wehrmacht into Holland and Belgium on 10 May.

By Mistake on Purpose

In the Norwegian Corridor German and Swedish ships were supplying the Third Reich with vital mineral ores for their armaments manufacture. So Churchill wrote to the First Sea Lord in March 1940: 'Would it not be possible

Right: Winston Churchill examining a tommy-gun during a visit to North-East England.

In April 1940, there was a minor reconstruction in the Government and Neville Chamberlain took the opportunity of putting Winston Churchill at the head of a committee of Service Ministers for the purpose of guiding the conduct of the war. His energy and military knowledge made it a very popular appointment.

Below: The *Daily Mirror*, 8 April 1940. A totalitarian eclipse has been arranged.

On 4th April a statement was issued from 10 Downing Street that the First Lord of the Admiralty, as the Senior Service Minister, would preside over the Military Co-ordination Committee. This gave the Press and public fresh confidence.

to have one or two merchant ships of sufficient speed, specially strengthened in the bows and equipped with a ram. These vessels would carry merchandise and travel up to the heads [sheltered waters around the Norwegian ports] looking for German ore ships or any other German merchant vessels and then ram them by accident.' By mistake on purpose ...

Walking with Destiny

Neville Chamberlain stepped down as Prime Minister in May 1940. He, the majority of the Conservative party and King George VI preferred Lord Halifax (Edward Frederick Lindley Wood, 1st Earl of Halifax), who was at the time Secretary of State for Foreign Affairs, to succeed. Halifax refused, ostensibly because as a member of the House of Lords there would be practical and constitutional difficulties. So the sixty-five-year-old Churchill accepted the King's commission to form a new government — on 10 May. Hitler chose that day to launch his Panzers in the blitzkrieg against Belgium, Holland and France. It seemed fateful. Churchill now believed that he was walking with destiny.

Captain of the ship, May 1940.

"*Two gun Winston*"; The *Daily Mail*, 13 May 1940. On 11 May 1940 Winston Churchill formed a new Government, with himself as Prime Minister and Minister of Defence.

The Cat among the Pigeons

When Churchill became Prime Minister in May 1940 there was dismay in Whitehall, and disappointment in Westminster. Jock Colville, who later became a trusted private secretary, wrote: 'The mere thought of Churchill as Prime Minister sent a cold chill down the spines of the staff at 10 Downing Street where I was working as Assistant Private Secretary to Mr Neville Chamberlain. Churchill's impetuosity had, we thought, contributed to the Norwegian fiasco and General Ismay had told us in despairing tones of the confusions caused by his enthusiastic irruptions into the peaceful and orderly deliberations of the Military Co-ordinating Committee and the Chiefs of Staff. His verbosity and restlessness made unnecessary work, prevented real planning and caused friction.'

The cat among the pigeons?

Churchill's National Coalition

Churchill brought with him from the Admiralty his principal private secretary, Eric Seal, and also John Peck. Jock Colville went to Admiralty House 'where Winston proposes to work at night. He has fitted up the ground floor for this purpose: the dining-room in which the private secretary and one of Winston's specially trained night-women-typists sit; the lovely drawing room ... used as a kind of promenade; and an inner room in which the Great Man himself sits. At the side of his desk stands a table laden with bottles of whisky, etc. On the desk itself are all manner of things: toothpicks, gold medals (which he uses as paper-weights), special cuffs to save his coat sleeves from becoming dirty, and innumerable pills and powders.' The War Cabinet of five appointed by Churchill included Clement Attlee, Arthur Greenwood, both Labour; and Halifax, A. V. Alexander, First Lord of the Admiralty, and Anthony Eden. There were senior posts for Ernest Bevin, Herbert Morrison and Hugh Dalton. Kingsley Wood became Chancellor of the Exchequer and Chamberlain Lord President of the Council. It was a genuine National Coalition of the three main political parties.

Wehrmacht soldiers enter France, May 1940.

'Blood, Toil, Tears and Sweat'

On 13 May 1940, three days after Hitler launched his devastating blitzkrieg against Belgium, France and Holland, Churchill made an exceptional speech in the House of Commons. 'I would say to the House ... "I have nothing to offer but blood, toil, tears and sweat" ... You ask, what is our policy? I can say: It is to wage war, by sea, land and air, with all our might and with all the strength that God can give us; to wage war against a monstrous tyranny, never surpassed in the dark, lamentable catalogue of human crime ... You ask, what is our aim? I can answer in one word: It is victory, victory at all costs, victory in spite of all terror ... for without victory, there is no survival ... no survival for the British Empire ...'

Truly, a heart-warming, exuberant speech that cheered the nation. As he sat down, there was a moment of stunned silence followed by a magnificent standing ovation. The stage was set for the dramas that lay ahead.

France: a Fight to the Bitter End?

The Dutch Government surrendered on 14 May 1940 and the Belgians on the 27th. Boulogne was captured on the 23rd and Calais at the end of the month. Churchill was desperate to help and to encourage France to keep on fighting. He visited Paris several times. 'I have received from the Chief of the French Republic [Paul Reynaud, their Prime Minister] the most sacred pledges that whatever happens they will fight to the end be it bitter or be it glorious.' He and everyone else thought that the French Army was the most powerful in Europe, perhaps in the world. He offered them a 'Declaration of Union'. On 31 May Churchill flew to Tours with Clement Attlee (Lord Privy Seal), General Sir John Dill (the new Chief of the Imperial General Staff), General Edward Spears and General 'Pug' Ismay (Military Secretary to the Committee of Imperial Defence). They were met by Reynaud, General Maxime Weygand (Supreme Commander in Gamelin's wake) and a dejected old man who turned out to be Marshal Pétain (who surrendered the French Army ignominiously on 18 June). It was to no avail. Paris fell without a fight on the 14th and Hitler was soon marching down the Champs-Élysees. Another tragedy was that of the surrounding and capture of the 5lst Highland Division at St-Valéry-en-Caux. Technically under French Army command, cries of 'Albion perfide' would have been uttered if the Scots were to rejoin British command and escape. It was a catastrophe. Soon the hostile Vichy France came into being.

Operation Dynamo: Dunkirk Rescue

The British Expeditionary Force made a fighting retreat to the only Channel port not in enemy hands — Dunkirk. Adolf Hitler trusted Goering's promise that his Luftwaffe would demolish Allied forces hemmed in around the port and along the beaches. He restrained his Panzer divisions for a variety of reasons. Admiral Ramsay and the Royal Navy, backed by hundreds of small private yachts, tugs, trawlers and ferries succeeded in Operation Dynamo in rescuing 338,000 troops (of which 110,000 were French and Polish). This was more than 85 per cent of the BEF. It was nine days and nights of heroism. The Royal Navy's 220 vessels suffered heavily from Stuka bombers as the RAF had of course to operate from British aerodromes. Bringing to a close another great speech in the House of Commons, Churchill noted on 4 June 1940, the final day: 'We must be very careful not to assign to this deliverance the attributes of a victory. Wars are not won by evacuation ... We shall go on to the end. We shall fight in France. We shall fight on the seas and oceans ... We shall never surrender.'

The *Daily Express*, 8 June 1940.

Lofty Calm?

Churchill drove himself and everyone he could extremely hard. They were sad, dangerous days. But Clementine, who had heard complaints of her husband's impatience and overbearing and contemptuous manners, took him to task and wrote to him (from Downing Street on 27 June 1940), sweetly and apologetically, but firmly. She pointed out to him that he gave the orders and had the authority to sack anyone, except the King, the Archbishop of Canterbury and the Speaker, if those orders were not carried out to his liking. With this great power he had, she told him, he should combine kindness, courtesy and lofty calm — this was much more likely to get the desired results than displays of temper and offensive behaviour, which would make him disliked and lose him support.

'Crusade ... With a Band of Privateers'

Jock Colville was a dedicated Churchill-watcher. In late May 1940 he wrote: 'Our fortunes are at a low ebb ... In any case, whatever Winston's shortcomings, he seems to be the man for the occasion. His spirit is indomitable and even if France and England should be lost, I feel he would carry on the crusade himself with a band of privateers.'

A Hurricane being re-armed during the Battle of Britain.

Carting Bombs into Germany

It was Professor Lindemann's opinion after the collapse of France that effectively the German food problems would be resolved. Churchill was perturbed: 'It seems to me that the blockade [of Germany] is largely ruined, in which case the sole decisive weapon in our hands would be overwhelming air attack upon Germany.' He warned the Cabinet on 3 September 1940, towards the end of the Battle of Britain, that 'the [RAF] fighters are now our salvation but the bombers alone can provide the means of victory' The RAF bombing raids by day soon suffered unacceptable losses. 'On no account should the limited bomber force be diverted from accurate bombing of military objectives reaching far into Germany. Is it not possible to organize a Second Line Bomber force (Lysanders, etc.); the Ruhr is a prime target.' He then asked for a wholehearted effort 'to cart a large number of bombs into Germany by the Second Line Organization' — a rather impractical plan to use planes (such as Lysanders) that were not designed as bombers to carry out bombers' tasks. Lord Dowding (Hugh Dowding, Air Chief Marshal of the RAF and Commander-in-Chief of Fighter Command) thought that 'the race to destroy the other's aircraft industry will imply bombing the civilian population. Then the real test will begin; have we or the Germans the sterner civilian morale?'

The Artful Dodger

Churchill had been in touch with Franklin Delano Roosevelt, the US President, since 11 September 1939. Once described as an 'artful dodger', FDR was a curious mixture, ruthless but charming, cynical but soft, vindictive but loyal. He certainly regarded British imperialism with suspicion, even hostility, but he knew that without American help and forces the war could not be won. Britain was utterly alone after the fall of France. Despite many visits, exhortations and pleading, only limited US help was forthcoming as Britain struggled. The unhelpful, biased US Ambassador, Joseph Kennedy, was convinced that Britain was doomed. Even when Hitler's U-boats were sinking merchant ships off the American eastern seaboard with apparent impunity, FDR knew that Congress would not countenance war with Germany. Churchill tried his best, but was stymied by the US Congress.

'Patience is a Virtue'

'His anger was like lightning and sometimes terrifying to see, but it lasted a short time,' wrote Jock Colville. 'He could be violently offensive to those who worked for him and although he would never say he was sorry, he would equally never let the sun go down without in some way making amends or showing that he had not meant to be unkind. His sarcasm could be biting, but it was often accompanied by an engaging smile which seemed to say that no harm was really intended. He had a great liking for young people ... and he treated his Secretariat as if they were his children. He was not easy to work for, particularly during the anxious days of the war. Patience is a virtue with which he was totally unfamiliar.'

Boniface and the 'Magic Circle'

The secret decoding establishment at Bletchley Park, 60 miles north-west of London, was set up to decipher radio messages enciphered on the Enigma machine (a complex device that encrypted and decrypted messages) used by the German armed forces, the Abwehr, SS and the railway system. Thanks to the bravery of the Poles and the French, captured Enigma machines were installed for geniuses such as Alan Turing, Bill Tutte, John Tiltman and Max Newman to break the 'impossible' German codes. On 22 May 1940 they broke the main Luftwaffe operational key. Churchill called the intercepts the 'Golden eggs' and personally code-named his daily input 'Operation Boniface'.

Brigadier Stewart Menzies, head of MI6 (known as 'C') delivered each day to No. 10 Downing Street ancient buff-coloured boxes marked VRI (which stood for *Victoria Regina et Imperatrix* — 'Victoria, Queen and Empress'). The PM kept the only key. The Free French were not told the secret of Ultra (the code word for the Bletchley Park decrypts), nor were the Russians, nor were the Americans until they entered the fray. The 100,000 Enigma machines used by the Wehrmacht, the Luftwaffe and the German state rail network, the Reichsbahn, were providing hundreds of radio messages each day. The German naval signals were mastered early in 1941 and the Wehrmacht's in 1942. On his wartime travels Churchill met many of the Bletchley Park Special Liaison Officers and sergeants who received the decrypts and carefully briefed their military superiors. He called them 'The Magic Circle'. None of his Private Secretaries were privy to Boniface. Nobody knew at the time, in 1935, that Beobachter-Dienst, the German code-breaking service, had broken the Royal Navy convoy ciphers. Admiral Raeder of the German Navy was delighted at this — but he did not know that his HYDRA, NEPTUN, SUD and MEDUSA naval cipher codes were being decrypted by Ultra and Bletchley Park!

The Local Defence Volunteers (afterwards the Home Guard) were formed in May 1940 to repel a German invasion. "A force," said Churchill, "of more than a million and a half who are determined to fight for every inch of the ground in every village and every street."

Operation Catapult

This naval battle to capture or destroy the French fleet at Mers-el-Kebir, near Oran in Algeria, was for Churchill a dreadful decision to have to make, but it was vital that the Germans should not seize the modern battle-cruisers *Dunkerque* and *Strasbourg*, under the command of Admiral Gensoul. The Royal Navy Gibraltar squadron under Vice-Admiral Somerville — known as Force H — a powerful force, would present three alternatives to the French: that they fight the Germans and Italians alongside the British; that they sail their vessels to a British port; or that they sail their vessels to a French port in the West Indies. Negotiations failed and a terrible naval action took place on 3 July 1940. A ten-minute bombardment followed by air attacks from *Ark Royal* resulted in all the French vessels except one being sunk or put out of action; 1,200 French sailors lost their lives. French ships in Alexandria and other ports were also put out of action. The message rang around the world — to Germany and the USA, that 'Britain was fighting for her life and the British War Cabinet would stop at nothing.'

The Battle of Britain and Operation Sealion

Hitler ordered the first stage of Operation Sealion, the invasion of Britain, on 10 July 1940. Many thousands of barges and small craft clustered in all the Channel ports and harbours waiting for the second stage. Marshal Goering, having failed to demolish the BEF at Dunkirk, made another rash promise to his Führer, that his Luftwaffe would destroy the RAF, in the air and on the ground, in what became known as 'The Battle of Britain'. Once the RAF was neutralized, the Royal Navy warships should then be at the mercy of the dreaded Stuka dive-bombers. The Luftwaffe had gathered 2,669 operational aircraft (1,308 fighters and 1,361 bombers) and on 5 August the Führer's Directive No. 17 authorized the intensified air war. The RAF had an operational fighter strength that varied from 603 to 722. The Battle of Britain lasted for six weeks. The RAF pilots included Poles, Canadians, Australians, New Zealanders, Free French and a few Americans. They were magnificent in the air. Anti-aircraft batteries defended the airfields and the cities, and the fire brigades fought the blazing wrecked houses and factories. The daily score of planes downed was broadcast by the BBC and followed by everyone. For a variety of reasons the 'home side' figures were rather optimistic. In mid-August the air battles reached a frenzied climax. Air Chief Marshal Lord Dowding had to keep back a small reserve to deal with the invasion fleets. Finally on 17 September Hitler called off Operation Sealion. The actual figures of losses (missing or complete write-offs) were somewhat exaggerated. The RAF claimed they had shot down 2,698 Luftwaffe — later

A Luftwaffe bomber over the Surrey Docks, London, September 1940.

investigation showed that they had downed 1,733; the Germans claimed they had shot down 3,058 aircraft — the actual number was 915. Hitler then authorized Goering to blitz London and other cities and destroy the civilian resistance. Churchill's famous phrase praised the young heroes: 'Never in the field of human conflict was so much owed by so many to so few.'

London Blitz

The Luftwaffe bombing of London at the end of August 1940 marked the start of tit-for-tat bombing, Churchill sending the RAF to Berlin to make a retaliatory raid. Hitler countered this by stating, on 4 September, 'If they attack our cities, we will simply erase theirs' — as the Luftwaffe had already done in the Netherlands. From 7 February to 3 November an average of 200 Luftwaffe bombers attacked London every night. But, as Churchill noted, the city seemed capable of surviving the most horrific of injuries and lived on, half-ruined, in spite of its wounds.

'Give 'Em Socks'

Colin Perry, aged eighteen, was working for an oil company in Lothbury in the City of London when the Blitz started in early September 1940. At lunchtime on Tuesday the 10th, he found 'Cheapside a mass of charred debris; of firemen on ladders, hoses pouring jets of water into the burning remains of elegant buildings of yesterday. Fire units, engines, troops in steel helmets move in the dense choking clouds of smoke rising high above St Paul's. Near Mansion House tube station a huge crowd gathered. "Winston Churchill!" I cheered, I yelled. I fought hard and finally established myself next to Churchill. Once I had my hand on his coat. He looked invincible, which he is. Tough, bulldogged, piercing. His hair was wispy, wiry, tinted gingery. As he made his way through the smoke, through the City workers, all crying "Good old Winston" — "give 'em socks" — "Good luck" ... It was magnificent, tremulous, stirring, dramatic.

Amongst the "ashes of London" stepped the man, his people, acclaimed, assured, and fulfilling the declaration that we will fight in the streets, in the fields, on the seas, in the air — that we should rather see London in ashes, but free and ours, than standing under the will of Hitler ... Winston stood on the bomb crater, waved, took off his bowlerish hat, sporting his walking-stick ... '

A Luftwaffe bomber is show down in London. The major raids occurred between 7 September 1940 and 16 May 1941. London was bombed on 57 consecutive nights.

Lend-Lease: Elderly American Destroyers

When Italy came into the war in May 1940, its huge submarine fleet might have destroyed the balance of control which the Royal Navy held in the Mediterranean. There was also a production gap in British shipyards to replace the grievous losses in Operation Dynamo and in the earlier Norwegian campaign. Churchill spent months negotiating a complicated deal with President Roosevelt. Their correspondence was from 'Former Naval Person' to 'Colonel Knox' and resulted in the supply of fifty 'reconditioned' unwanted American destroyers to the Royal Navy. In return, a ninety-nine-year lease was granted to the USA for the establishment of naval and air bases (on their doorstep) in Newfoundland, Bermuda, Bahamas, Jamaica, Antigua, St Lucia, Trinidad and British Guiana. And a guarantee that if Britain was overrun the British Fleet would never be surrendered or scuttled. 'They [the destroyers] proved to be of vital assistance in the forthcoming Battle of the Atlantic against the U-boats.' This was true but forty of the old ladies needed restoration before, early in 1941, they took to the high seas.

HMS Churchill

PM to Captain HM Destroyer *Churchill*: 'Am delighted that your ship should be named after the great Duke of Marlborough and I am sending you one of his handwritten letters for your Ward Room for luck.' 25 September 1940.

'Coventrated' and the 'Baedecker Raids'

Hitler kept his dreadful promise; 500 Luftwaffe bombers shattered Coventry on 14 November. The Germans invented a new word — 'Coventrated' — probably first used by the execrable Lord Haw-Haw (William Joyce), the renegade British broadcaster in Berlin. Then followed raids on Birmingham (19-22 November), Bristol, Southampton, Liverpool, Plymouth, Sheffield, Manchester, Leeds and Glasgow which all suffered blitzes in what the media called the 'Baedecker Raids' (from the name of the German tourist guidebook to historic places of interest).

Churchill worked in the underground Cabinet HQ at Storey's Gate, Westminster, close to the entrance to St James's Park. No. 10 Downing Street was damaged by bombs in the London Blitz. However, from the Downing Street Annexe, an exceedingly strong building, at night Churchill walked on it to watch the bombing of London, usually wearing his well-known 'Rompers' or 'Siren Suit' and over them a multi-coloured dressing gown.

Deaths from the Luftwaffe bombing came to between 3,000 and 5,000 per month. When the RAF sent two hundred bombers on Operation Abigail to do a 'Coventry' on Mannheim, thirty-four civilians were killed and seven bombers were lost.

Drizzle of Carping Criticism

Since time began newly elected governments have had a honeymoon period before, for a variety of reasons, disenchantment sets in. In November 1940 Winston Churchill had need to proffer advice to the Prime Minister of New Zealand. 'We dwell under a drizzle of carping criticism from a few Members and from writers in certain organs of the Press. This has an irritating effect and would not be tolerated in any other country exposed to our present stresses. On the other hand, it is a good thing that any Government should be kept keen and made aware of any shortcomings in time to remedy them. You must not suppose everything is perfect, but we are trying our best.'

Winston Churchill keeps the King informed on all aspects of the war.

The Wizard War

The period after the Battle of Britain was called by Churchill the 'Wizard War' — a war whose battles were fought in secret, hardly understood even afterwards. It was like *Star Wars*. Radio beams guided Luftwaffe bombers to their nocturnal targets in Britain. The British boffins countered with 'meacons' which picked up the German beams and diverted them. Then the Germans came up with *Knickebein*, an invisible searchlight beam for their bombers. Once Churchill understood the issue, he wrote later, he ordered that priority should be given to developing counter-measures. The Knickebein stations near Dieppe and Cherbourg then had their beams jammed or diverted. And so it went on with the German X, then Y apparatus (radio beams with a range finder which 'told' the Luftwaffe bomber pilot when the correct distance to its target had been reached) — new counter-measures were introduced. The Luftwaffe bombing of Dublin on 30 May 1941 was probably a diverted Y-apparatus attack.

Winston Churchill was always on the move, to see things for himself and to motivate. Here at Southampton Docks he is meeting sixteen-year-old Georgie Smith, the youngest worker in the dockyard.

'Set Europe Ablaze'

Churchill gave the Labour politician Hugh Dalton authority to cobble together from MIR (Military Intelligence Research), EH ('Electra House', discreet propaganda section of the Foreign Office) and Section D (which studied sabotage) of the SIS (Secret Intelligence Service, better known now as MI6), a small organization — the Special Operations Executive, or SOE — to 'set Europe ablaze'. The methods it used included industrial and military sabotage, labour agitation and strikes, continuous propaganda, terrorist acts against traitors and German leaders, boycotts and riots. Brigadier Colin Gubbins, as head of operations, had to battle in Europe, as well as with the SIS who viewed their new rivals with disdain and alarm. The first operation was by parachute into Poland; then Spain (bribery to keep Franco's army out of the war); Operation Claymore (to capture Enigma material) in the Lofoten islands; Rubble (escape of Norwegian ships with vital steel supplies); Relator (plan for guerrilla war in Spain); Savanna (tackling the Luftwaffe's Kampf Geschwader bomber squadrons in Brittany); Marchioness (sabotaging a Japanese ship in Lisbon); Irongates (oil tankers in Romania); a coup in Belgrade, Pickaxe (twenty-five Soviet agents into Allied Europe); and so on. Arming and helping lead the French Maquis in their resistance movements was perhaps SOE's greatest triumph, sadly offset by disaster in Holland when the Abwehr reeled in forty of its agents.

May the Many Owe Much to *These* Few. *The Daily Mail*, 4 October 1940. The Battle of Britain was at its height, depending almost entirely upon its airmen—the First of the Few. The War Cabinet included Mr C. R. Attlee, the Labour leader, Mr Arthur Greenwood, Lord Halifax, Lord Beaverbrook, Sir John Anderson, Mr Ernest Bevin and Sir Kingsley Wood. Note how diminutively Lord Beaverbrook — the owner of the competitor newspaper, *The Daily Express* — is represented in the cartoon.

The Crucial Vote of Confidence

During 1940 the British Army in North Africa under General Wavell, aided by Australian, New Zealand, South African and Indian formations, crippled Mussolini's gigantic forces. Libya, Sollum, Bardia, Tobruk, Benghazi were taken one after another. The Italians were also beaten in Somaliland and Eritrea. The Royal Navy had a convincing victory at Taranto, destroying one Italian battleship and severely damaging two others and other craft. Malta was bombed daily. It was a honeymoon period. And it didn't last: Churchill ordered British and Commonwealth troops into Greece, which were then overwhelmed by Panzers and Stukas; and Hitler sent General Rommel with a Panzer force into North Africa, which was more than a match for the Allied forces in 1941 and 1942. By 24 April 1941 Greece had surrendered and Crete followed suit to a German paratroop battle group after a heroic battle. Churchill asked the House of Commons for a Vote of Confidence on 7 May 1941, which he won by 447 votes to 3. He said, 'The loss of the Nile Valley and Suez Canal and the loss of our position in the Mediterranean, the loss of Malta would be among the heaviest blows which we could sustain.' He reminded the house that

The Depth Charge. The *Daily Mail*, 6 December 1940. The Prime Minister is personally devoting himself to the problem of beating the U-boat.

General Wavell had 500,000 troops under his command. Having previously offered nothing but blood, tears, toil and sweat, 'I will now add our fair share of mistakes, shortcomings and disappointments ... We have no need to fear the tempest. Let it roar, and let it rage. We shall come through.'

The Bismarck is Sunk

At the end of May 1941, the new ultra-fast, ultra-powerful German battleship, the *Bismarck*, was hunted down and finally sunk. It was sailing from Bergen in Norway through the Denmark Strait, apparently heading for Brest or Saint-Nazaire. Single-handed it could have destroyed British convoys. It was met by the twenty-three-year-old HMS *Hood*, the fastest capital ship in the world, which was sunk with the loss of all but a few of the crew. All in Britain held their breath as the Royal Navy sought revenge. The battleship *Prince of Wales* and the aircraft carriers *Victorious* and *Ark Royal* tracked the great German ship. Destroyers fired torpedoes. Fleet Air Arm planes bombed. The *Prince of Wales* shelled. Eventually the *Bismarck*, having put up a tremendous fight, was sunk and Churchill, who was intensely gloomy after Rommel's African successes, the loss of Crete and the sinking of the *Hood*, was cheered up by the dramatic end to the powerful *Bismarck*.

The Kremlin and the Führer

Churchill had always been vehemently anti-Communist and this hatred increased following the German-Russian non-aggression pact of 1939. After the fall of France, Stalin and Molotov were delighted that the unhappy Baltic states fell into their hands and Poland was divided with Germany. The Kremlin congratulated the Führer on each of his victories. Their radio programmes slandered and abused Great Britain. Their Fifth Column Communists tried to cause unrest and trouble in British factories. Churchill was to write, however, that, cunning and brutal as he was, Stalin showed a surprising lack of understanding and foresight about what was in store for his country and remained blind to his new German friend's plans right up to the moment of Hitler's assault in June 1941.

KMS *Bismarck* and her sister ship *Tirpitz* were the largest battleships built by Germany. During the fight with HMS *Hood* and HMS *Prince of Wales* the *Bismarck* was hit three times and suffered a ruptured oil tank. Two days later *Bismarck* was attacked by Swordfish from HMS *Ark Royal*, damaging the steering gear. The following day she was attacked by several British ships; HMS *King George V*, HMS *Rodney*, and the cruiser HMS *Dorsetshire*. *Bismarck* sank on 26 May 1941 with 114 survivors from a crew of 2,200.

'Clumsily Cooked-up Propaganda'

Station X's ULTRA (decrypting German Enigma messages) at Bletchley Park had picked up many clues that pointed to an invasion of Russia by Hitler. Airfield runways were being extended for Luftwaffe bombers. Wehrmacht divisions were massing on the Russian frontiers. Motorized and tank formations were moved into position. Churchill asked Sir Alexander Cadogan of the Foreign Office to brief the Soviet Ambassador, Maysky, about the detailed German forces, without of course, specifying the source: 'The PM asks you urgently to communicate all these data to the Soviet Government.' This was on 10 June, twelve days before the Nazi offensive code-named Operation Barbarossa. Four days later, the Soviet News Agency Communiqué referred to 'clumsily cooked-up propaganda' and affirmed that 'Germany is unswervingly observing the conditions of the Soviet-German Pact of Non-Aggression.' A week later the non-aggressive Panzer tanks, artillery, Stukas, SS (*Schutzstaffel*) and Wehrmacht launched into 'Barbarossa'.

Winston Churchill
stands amid the
rubble of the House
of Commons,
11 May 1941.

The New Ally

On 22 June 1941 Churchill broadcast a speech to the nation concerning Hitler's invasion of Russia, emphasizing that Russia's danger was Britain's danger, and that of the United States.

Stalin sent Ambassador Ivan Maysky with demands for military diversions by British forces and Churchill sent Beaverbrook to Moscow, who came back a champion of 'Aid to Russia' — aid for their new ally, until so recently chummy with the Führer and indifferent to Britain's survival. Churchill advised Beaverbrook to be careful that the British were not taken advantage of. The official minute in mid-August was more tactful, greeting Russia as a welcome guest. 'Uncle Joe' wanted a Second Front in the Balkans or France which would draw off thirty to forty Wehrmacht divisions, and requested 30,000 tons of aluminium and a *monthly* supply of 400 aircraft and 500 tanks.

Twenty-five to thirty-five British divisions could be sent either by sea to Archangel (braving the U-boat packs) or overland by train to Basra (Iraq) to the Caspian, suggested Stalin. Even so, 'Aid to Russia' convoys sailed every ten days with tanks and aircraft for Britain's bad-tempered and demanding new ally.

An RAF Sunderland overlooks a convoy on the Western Approaches. The first British convoy had sailed to Russia on 21 August 1941. The most dangerous part of the voyage began with the passage north of Norway. From that point, for the remainder of the journey through the Barents Sea the ships were within reach of Luftwaffe, U-boats and destroyers based in the north of Norway and Finland. To add some protection, some RAF units were operated from Russian soil.

American Relationships

The bloody-minded US Ambassador Joseph Kennedy had been recalled to the USA and was replaced by John Gilbert Winant. He was staunchly pro-British and was quickly absorbed into Churchill's inner circle, where he promptly fell in love with Sarah Churchill. Other influential Americans at Churchill's 'court' were the diplomat Hershel Johnson, the politician and diplomat Averell Harriman and, particularly, Roosevelt's adviser, Harry Hopkins. In July there were significant meetings with the Americans in London about aircraft, tanks, food supplies, munitions and convoy protection. Chartwell was closed for the war. Chequers was a possible Luftwaffe target and so the 'court' moved to Ditchley, the palatial Oxfordshire country house of one of Churchill's friends, fellow Anglo-American, Ronald Tree, Conservative MP for Market Harborough. Churchill spent fifteen weekends there in 1941-2. He was determined to meet President Roosevelt and sailed across the Atlantic aboard HMS *Prince of Wales* to Placentia Bay off Newfoundland. On 12 August they signed the historic 'Atlantic Charter'. The rather imprecise eight-page document did not commit Roosevelt, but it was a blueprint for a better world, and later formed the basis of the United Nations Declaration. And the two great men, FDR and WSC, met for only the second time since their brief introduction to each other back in 1919. For their chiefs of staff, Dill and Marshall, it was their first meeting.

A Day in the Country

On 26 September 1941 Churchill visited devastated Coventry and its
cathedral, and toured the Armstrong-Siddeley factory, where torpedoes and
aircraft parts were made. In every workshop the men clanged their hammers
in a deafening welcome. Then to the Whitley bomber factory which was a
hotbed of Communism. The PM's appearance, with cigar and 'semi-top-hat',
captivated the workers who gave him vociferous applause. A new Whitley
took off and flew past, a Hurricane pilot did stunts and No. 605 squadron of
Hurricanes flew over in astonishingly tight formation. The men and women of
the factory quite forgot their Communism and rushed forward in serried ranks
to say goodbye. Their production had only really grown since Russia came into
the war. Churchill's party visited a cemetery where Coventry's air-raid dead
were buried. Then to Birmingham to visit a tank factory and a Spitfire works
at Castle Bromwich. Everywhere the crowds gave Churchill a tumultuous
welcome, cheering and shouting with joy.

Lunching at County Hall, London, 14 July 1941 Churchill declared "*We live in a terrible epoch of the human story, but we believe there is a broad and sure justice running through its theme. It is time that the Germans should be made to suffer in their own homeland and cities something of the torment they have twice in our lifetime let loose upon their neighbours and upon the world. We have now intensified for a month past our systematic, scientific, methodical bombing on a large scale of the German cities, seaports, industries, and other military objectives. We believe it to be in our power to keep this going, on a steadily rising tide, month after month, year after year, until the Nazi regime is either extirpated by us, or better still, torn to pieces by the German people themselves.*"

Where is Tirpitz?

Launched in 1939, a sister ship to the *Bismarck*, the *Tirpitz* was more heavily armed, better protected, faster, and could travel greater distances without refuelling than any Royal Navy battleship. In January 1942 Winston Churchill remarked that the crippling of the *Bismarck* would alter the entire face of the naval war and that the loss of 100 aircraft and 500 airmen would be well compensated for.

Between October 1940 and her eventual sinking in November 1944, there were no fewer than 24 major sea and air attempts to sink *Tirpitz*. The key effort to disable her was by six midget submarines late in September 1943. Churchill followed closely all the brave efforts to keep that Leviathan of the seas immobilised.

The Prime Minister with pilots of 615 Fighter Squadron during a visit to RAF Manston, Kent, on 25 September 1941.

Hitler's Table Talk: 'Most Bloodthirsty'

'Churchill is determined to continue air warfare. We are also resolved to continue and are preparing to drop 100 bombs for each British bomb until Britain gets rid of this criminal and his methods. Churchill is the most bloodthirsty of amateur strategists that history has ever known. He is as bad a politician as a soldier and as bad a soldier as a politician. Like a madman, Churchill has always been running all over Europe to look for a country to become a battlefield.' Speech by Hitler on 4 May 1941.

Hitler's Table Talk: 'Size of their Brains'

Entertaining Albert Speer (Nazi Germany's principal architect), and the sculptor Arno Breker on the evening of 18 October 1941, Adolf Hitler talked to them:

'It's a queer business, how England slipped into the war. The man who managed it was Churchill, that puppet of the Jewry that pulls the strings.

The Modern Icarus! The *Daily Mirror*, 12 November 1941. In mythical times Icarus and his father Daedalus attempted to fly from Crete to Italy, wearing wings fastened on by wax. Icarus soared so high that the sun melted the wax, and he fell into the sea, giving his name to that part of it.

Next to him, the bumptious Eden, a money-grubbing clown; the Jew who was Minister for War, Hore-Belisha; then the *Eminence grise* of the Foreign Office — and after that some other Jews and business men. With these last, it often happens that the size of their fortune is in inverse ratio to the size of their brains.'

Felines in the Family

Besides his wife, called by him Cat or Kat or Clem-Pussy-Bird, Pawser, Mrs Grimalkin, Churchill was genuinely fond of real felines. In June 1941 John Colville recorded how he had 'lunch alone with the PM and the Yellow Cat, which sat in a chair on his right-hand side and attracted most of his attention. While he brooded [on affairs of state], he kept up a running conversation with the cat, cleaning its eyes with his napkin, offering it mutton and expressing regret that it could not have cream in war-time.'

Nearing the Show-Down. The *Daily Mail*, 7 November 1941. After Germany's initial success in Russia, the tide of victory turned. Britain sent war supplies through Persia, and the severity of the Russian winter helped to defeat Hitler's troops.

The Greatest Joy: England Would Live

On Sunday evening, 7 December 1941, Churchill was conferring with the US Ambassador John Winant and Averell Harriman, Roosevelt's envoy to Britain. The BBC nine o'clock news carried a minor item; an attack by the Japanese on American shipping at Hawaii. Churchill immediately telephoned Roosevelt who confirmed a savage attack at Pearl Harbor. 'We are all in the same boat now,' said FDR. Hong Kong was attacked, and landings made in Malaya. The Prime Minister also learned that Hitler's armies had failed to capture Moscow and were struggling with 'General Winter'. Simultaneously, Hitler sided with Japan and declared war on America. Churchill greeted this with joy — it meant that the United States was now in the war, on the Allies' side. In the initial euphoria, it seemed to him that this meant victory, and that England would live.

USS *California* sinking after the Japanese surprise attack. *"Yesterday, Dec. 7, 1941 – a date which will live in infamy – the United States of America was suddenly and deliberately attacked by naval and air forces of the Empire of Japan.... The attack yesterday on the Hawaiian Islands has caused severe damage to American naval and military forces. Very many American lives have been lost."* President Franklin D Roosevelt's Pearl Harbor Speech to the Nation. 8 December 1941.

Operation Arcadia: 'Let Them Reap the Whirlwind'

On board HMS *Duke of York* (sister ship to the *Prince of Wales*, which had been sunk off the coast of Malaya by the Japanese on 9 December), Churchill and his entourage sailed across the Atlantic in Operation Arcadia, to the USA and Canada. Lodged with a personal retinue of five in the White House, Churchill spent two weeks as Roosevelt's guest. On Boxing Day 1941 he made his great speech to the joint session of both Houses of Congress. Having stressed his American family credentials, he went on to announce, 'I am a child of the House of Commons, brought up to believe in democracy.' He went on to praise the 'breadth of view and sense of proportion' he found in the United States, and the fortitude of the American people: 'After all, the United States have been attacked and set upon by three most powerfully armed dictator states. The greatest military power in Europe, the greatest military power in Asia, Germany and Japan, Italy too, have all declared, and are making, war upon you ... The forces ranged against us are enormous. They are bitter, they are ruthless ... They will stop at nothing.' Four days later he spoke in Ottawa to the Canadian Parliament: 'Hitler and his Nazi gang have sown the wind; let them reap the whirlwind.'

Over on the Bright Side! The *Daily Mail* 13 December 1941. The Japanese attacked the Americans at Pearl Harbor on 7 December, and Britain declared war on Japan the following day. But despite this bad news from the Pacific, there were advances on the Russian and Libyan fronts.

Churchill's Lion, Rota

On 11 August 1941 Churchill remarked with a touch of melancholy that his days of lion hunting were over. Like every titbit of his off-the-record conversation, the *mot* went through the entire British press. Mr George Thomson, a hunting gentleman in Kenya, read the lines. A few months later Rota arrived at Victoria Station, accompanied by her owner and two keepers. She was addressed to No. 10, but landed in the London Zoo, where she was the star attraction. Winston Churchill promised to return the fur of the British Empire's symbol after its death to her rightful owner.

Dinner at the White House

Eleanor Roosevelt, the President's wife, gave a dinner party at the White House on 13 January 1942. As well as Churchill, the guests included cousins of both the Roosevelts and the Yugoslavian-born American writer Louis Adamic and his wife. Not long afterwards, Adamic published a book entitled *Dinner at the White House*, based on that one evening. The whole book was anti-British and most certainly anti-Churchill, who took great umbrage and sued the author in the British courts. Eventually, five years later, on 15 January 1947 in the Kings Bench Division of the High Court of Justice, Churchill was awarded payment of a very substantial sum by way of damages plus a formal apology from the author.

During the North American trip Churchill travelled by train and he had a special carriage. Here he is seen working, reading dispatches in his sitting room on the train.

Prime Minister of Canada, William Lyon Mackenzie King, (1874-1950) with Roosevelt and Churchill on the terrace of the Citadel overlooking Quebec. The First Washington Conference (codenamed Arcadia) was held between 22 December 1941 and 14 January 1942. At the New Year Churchill was in Canada where highly satisfactory talks were held between the Anglo-Canadian War Cabinets. Canada was a major contributor to the war effort. William Mackenzie King was just 18 days younger than Churchill, having been born 17 December 1874.

Intrepid Airman

Churchill arrived in the USA on 22 December 1941 to have talks with the President. Admiral Doenitz alerted packs of U-boats to seek out and sink the battleship by which he would return to Britain.

Captain Kelly Rogers, a tall fair-haired Irish pilot of the giant flying boat *Berwick*, wrote: 'Dawn was breaking off the coast of Norfolk, Virginia when a naval launch came out to the flying boat. The Prime Minister, dressed in his siren suit, smiling happily and smoking a cigar, walked into the control deck after breakfast. We were about 8,000 feet up and above the clouds. He asked if he might take over the controls, settled into the pilot's seat, smiled broadly as he sent the £200,000 flying boat into a couple of steep turns. He then remarked casually that the aircraft was very different from a plane he had flown in 1913. Then the flight to Bermuda began ...'

Winston Churchill at the controls of the *Berwick*, January 1942.

Hitler's Table Talk: Churchill Out of Date

'Churchill is a man with an out-of-date political idea — that of the European balance of power. It no longer belongs to the sphere of realities. And yet it's because of this superstition that Churchill stirred England up to war. When Singapore falls Churchill will fall, too, I'm convinced of it.' 12–13 January 1942.

Singapore: a Catastrophe

Churchill, during his many years as the great war leader, had his share of military tragedies. And now Singapore ranked, almost, with the Dardanelles. For years he had been uneasy about the defences of the huge city-port: massive defences out to sea but little in front of an invader from the landward side. General Wavell, after visiting the garrison, wrote to Churchill on m February 1942, 'Morale of some troops is not good and none is as high as I should like to see.' Out of the garrison of 85,000, about 70,000 were fighting men, roughly two to one British and Australian. The city of Singapore sheltered a population of about a million of all races. Two out of three aerodromes on the island were within range of fire from the mainland across the Johore Strait. Since the end of 1941 Churchill had been demanding plans for the landward defences. When the Japanese invaders cut the water supply, which came from Johore on the mainland, defence became impossible. Four days after Wavell's visit, General Percival led his huge garrison into captivity and probable death. To Churchill the capture by the Japanese of this vital stronghold in the Far East was the most terrible military catastrophe in Britain's history. Goebbels, of course, gloated. 'For the first time in this war the English are obliged to hoist the white flag in grand style.'

'On the Toboggan'

Since the fiasco of the Norwegian campaign in 1940, the way the BEF were bundled out of France, and the failure in Greece, Crete, Tobruk and finally Singapore, Churchill had been secretly worried that British troops, man for man, were not as good as the Germans or Japanese. To Violet Bonham Carter, his clever, logical friend since 1906, he confided in February 1942 his 'fear that our soldiers are not as good fighters as their fathers were. In 1915 our men fought on even when they had only one shell left and were under a fierce barrage. Now they cannot resist dive-bombers. We have so many men in Singapore, so many men — they should have done better.' In his diary of 18 February, three days after the surrender at Singapore, the CIGS (Chief of the Imperial General Staff), Alan Brooke, wrote: 'Burma news bad. If the Army cannot fight better than it is doing at present we shall deserve to lose our Empire.' In March the Allied Army in Java laid down its arms. 'England,' declared Goebbels, 'is on the toboggan.'

Hitler's Table Talk: Churchill a 'Corrupt Journalist'

General Erwin Rommel, fresh from his victories in North Africa, was Hitler's dinner guest and was told: 'Churchill is the very type of a corrupt journalist. There's not a worse prostitute in politics. He himself has written that it's unimaginable what can be done in war with the help of lies. He's an utterly amoral, repulsive creature. I'm convinced that he has his place of refuge ready beyond the Atlantic. He obviously won't seek sanctuary in Canada. In Canada he'd be beaten up. He'll go to his friends the Yankees.' 18 February 1942.

Vyacheslav Mikhailovich Molotov, First Deputy Chairman of the Council of Ministers of the Soviet Union on a visit to London, May 1942.

HMS *Campbeltown* was originally US destroyer USS *Buchanan*, built 1918, transferred to the Royal Navy in 1940 as part of the 'Destroyers for Bases Agreement'. She was used in the St Nazaire Raid, and photographed here by the Germans, crashed into the lock gates, 28 March 1942.

Stalin, the Warrior Chief

The Russian Secretary, Vyacheslav Mikhaylovich Molotov, visited England in May 1942 and stayed with Churchill at Chequers. A twenty-year agreement of mutual assistance was duly signed. As the full weight of Hitler's Panzers and Stukas in Operation Barbarossa was savaging the Russian defences, Molotov pressed for a 'Second Front' in Europe. Churchill could promise nothing, but visited the Kremlin in Moscow in August. Four long, bruising meetings took place, with Russian insolence and insults making 'mutual assistance' difficult. However, in a broadcast in May 1942, Churchill praised the nation's steadfastness and courage under Stalin, its warrior chief. He compared the Russian people to the British — they would never give in but would fight on with undiminished courage.

Operation Jubilee

The brilliant, audacious, cross-Channel raid on Saint-Nazaire took place on 26 March 1942, when HMS *Campbeltown* (an old US destroyer) with 250 Commandos aboard, rammed, destroyed and blew up the great docks. The battle-cruiser *Tirpitz* and other large German Navy ships could not now be serviced. Plans were then made for a larger operation, initially called 'Rutter' and finally 'Jubilee'. The Canadian Army had been in the UK for several years and wanted action. The Allied military planners for the Second Front wanted to test a head-on full-scale (Navy, Army and Air Force) attack on a defended French port. Dieppe was chosen and on 19 August a force of 10,000 men, including 5,000 Canadians, 1,000 British commandoes, and 50 US Rangers, backed by substantial naval support and 56 RAF squadrons, fought bravely on the beaches. To no avail: the Dieppe garrison had been reinforced and were on full alert. It was a disaster — 4,384 out of the 6,086 who made it ashore were killed, wounded or captured. General Montgomery had advised beforehand that Jubilee should be cancelled. Churchill put a brave face on it, later writing that they were able to learn from their experience and build better craft. This was true and two years later in Overlord, brilliant, unusual equipment was deployed with success.

Tobruk Tragedy

Tobruk was the fortress-harbour linchpin of the North African coastal campaigns that since the end of 1939 had ebbed and flowed. Hitler sent a favourite general, Erwin Rommel, who had helped savage the British Expeditionary Force in 1940, to bolster the Italian forces on the Egyptian borders. In 1941 Tobruk, in Libya, was surrounded and survived a long siege successfully. But in June 1942 a short, sharp enemy attack by mainly German Panzers broke into the Tobruk defences and in a few days captured the garrison of 35,000. General Auchinleck had assured Churchill that forces and supplies in Tobruk were sufficient for a long siege. It was a humiliating defeat, to Churchill a devastating loss. Hitler was jubilant: 'The Eighth Army has been practically destroyed. In Tobruk the port installations are almost intact.' The booty accruing to Rommel included 10,000 cubic metres of petrol, rations and clothing to keep his troops going for many months to come.

'Baffled and Bewildered': Disagreeable Monty

After the capture of Tobruk, Churchill and the CIGS, Alan Brooke, were worried about the failure of the Eighth Army in North Africa, which, with overwhelming strength in men, guns, tanks, still could not hold its own against General Rommel's Afrika Korps. 'This splendid army, about double as strong as the enemy, is baffled and bewildered by its defeats. Rommel is living almost entirely on transport, and food and fuel captured from us ... his army's life hangs on a thread.' Churchill and Alan Brooke flew to Cairo and consulted all the key generals, admirals and air marshals. The choice of the new Eighth

Army Commander fell on William 'Strafer' Gott, noted for his courage, who was almost immediately killed. He was replaced by General Bernard Law Montgomery, new to the desert, who had done well with the BEF in 1940, and in the years to come never lost a battle. Claiming that Montgomery was familiar with desert warfare (which he was not), Churchill introduced him as courageous and dynamic, adding that if he was unpleasant to his acquaintances and subordinates — he was to the enemy, too. Churchill visited the front (9 August 1942) and saw the Alamein and Ruweisat positions (in Egypt) and was everywhere greeted with rapture by the troops. The choice of Montgomery was a great risk. Alan Brooke knew he was good and he was right.

Pooh Bear Humming 'We Are Here ...'

In June 1942 Churchill asked his CIGS, General Sir Alan Brooke, to accompany him in the Boeing Clipper, a huge flying boat, to meet the American commanders in the USA. Churchill was dressed in his zip-suit and zip-shoes with a black Homburg hat on the side of his head and his small gold-topped malacca cane in his hand. Alan Brooke recalled, 'Suddenly, almost like Pooh-Bear, he started humming, "We are here because we're here — we're here because we're here!" This little song could not have been more appropriate. It was at a time when the Atlantic had not been so very frequently flown, we were both doubtful why we were going, whether we should get there, what we would achieve while we were there, and whether we should ever get back.'

A 'Winne the Pooh' cartoon from 1936 when Winston Churchill was embroiled in the Abdication crisis. For cartoonists, the 'Winnie' connection was a great temptation.

Winterton's Nightmare. The *Evening Standard*, 21 May 1942. In a debate in the House of Commons on 21 May 1942 as to whether the war should be controlled by a committee of Chiefs of Staff headed by the Minister of Defence (Churchill) or whether it should be run by one man (Churchill) some Members of Parliament, including Earl Winterton, thought that the latter state existed already.

Alamein: the Great Desert Victory

In Egypt, aided by extensive secret information from Ultra, Montgomery won an important defensive victory at Alam el Halfa at the beginning of September and then for twelve days, from 28 October onwards, fought the terrible attritional second battle of El Alamein, code-named Lightfoot and Supercharge. The pursuit was slow, but four German and eight Italian divisions were smashed and 30,000 prisoners taken. Rommel's original tank force of 240 mustered only 38 on 5 November. He paid great credit to the British artillery. The Afrika Korps fought a dozen skilful delaying tactic battles including Mareth and Wadi Akarit before Tunis was captured jointly with Eisenhower's 'Torch' Armies. Alamein became a landmark, Churchill later remarking that the Allied forces had had no victories before it, and after the second battle of El Alamein suffered no defeats.

Churchill arrived in Moscow on 12 August 1942, and he knew the meeting would be difficult. Molotov had visited both London and Washington in May 1942, and when he returned to Moscow he had told Stalin that President Roosevelt had promised him that the Allies would open a 'second front' that year (by which the Soviets meant a D-Day type landing in northern France) in order to take pressure off the Red Army. But the American President had deliberately misled the Soviets. And the trouble was that Stalin was already distrustful of the Western Allies — this new broken 'promise' only added to that existing feeling.

Operation Torch

Operation Torch (originally Gymnast, then Super-Gymnast) was one of the most important in the Second World War. Russia was on the brink of surrender. The Germans were at the gates of Moscow and Stalingrad, and Stalin urgently needed a major campaign by the Allies to force Hitler to withdraw forces from his Eastern Front. In Moscow in August 1942 Churchill had told Stalin that a Second Front — the invasion of France — was, for many reasons, not possible. But Operation Torch, the capture of mainly French-held North Africa, including Casablanca, Oran, Algiers and eventually Tunis, by a gigantic American-British Army, interested Stalin. Rommel's troops would be taken from the rear; the French would fight Germans again; General Franco would almost certainly stay neutral; and the Italians would be put out of the war. General Eisenhower, a relatively unknown American commander, with two experienced British field officers, Anderson and Ramsay, was put in charge of the Army and Navy attacks east of the Straits of Gibraltar. Churchill gave nicknames to the two US generals responsible for the western sector around Casablanca — Mark Clark was the 'American Eagle' and Bedell Smith the 'American Bulldog'.

There were many imponderables. The American forces had to cross the Atlantic, which was swarming with U-boats. The French might decide to fight vigorously to defend their territory. Spain might just decide to capture Gibraltar, the key port for the British forces. Hitler might get wind of Torch and deploy the Luftwaffe to destroy the huge convoys of American and British forces preparing for the 8 November 1942 landings. Churchill told Eden that if the operation failed he would resign. But, in the end, after many vicissitudes, Torch was successful, and all the Allied Armies, including General Montgomery's, converged on Tunis and a quarter of a million German troops were captured.

Churchill at the Casablanca Conference (code-named 'Symbol'), 14-23 January 1943.

Churchill aboard a ship *en route* to the Casablanca Conference.

The French Affair

Generals De Gaulle and Giraud were competing in North Africa to be the leaders of the Free French forces. They came fairly reluctantly to the top-level Casablanca conference on 24 January 1943. Churchill noted that many of the Frenchmen were far more concerned with their personal positions and power than with fighting for their country's freedom — indeed, they seemed to hate one another far more than they did the Germans. He remarked that when disaster befalls a country, it attracts further ills.

Operation Husky: Mount Etna and Malaria

The Casablanca Conference in January 1943 agreed to Operation Husky, the invasion and capture of Sicily, as a stepping stone into Italy. Huge armadas and convoys of troops, immense air bombardments and parachute drops took place on 10 July. General Patton's Seventh Army landed on the west coast, Montgomery's Eighth Army in the south. Thereafter it was a race to get to Messina and to sight the Italian mainland. The Germans reinforced their defences with the 1st Parachute Division, which held up the British attack. Patton's advance guard reached Messina on 16 August. The Italian defenders lost 130,000, mainly taken as prisoners of war, and the Germans 37,000. The Allied casualties were 31,000. Churchill, in Canada at the time, at the Quadrant conference, pronounced himself pleased with the result of the 38-day campaign. It had been slow and difficult, with Mount Etna blocking the Eighth Army's way, while at the same time providing a good location for the enemy from which to watch their movements. What's more, the PM pointed out, the forces had also to contend with malaria as they crossed the Catania plain towards Etna. They were unable to prevent the German evacuation to the mainland but the capture of Sicily opened the way for the Allied incursion into Italy.

The Big Order

Guy Eden was an expert Churchill watcher and saw him at close quarters during the war years: 'no doubting that this was, indeed, the supreme period of his life'.

As the wartime Prime Minister Churchill found extreme satisfaction in being able to wield the broadest brush and to plan on a scale satisfying even to him. The egotism he never tried to conceal was given full play. Orders and objurgations, code-names and encouragements flowed ceaselessly from his

Churchill examines closely the new rifle and short bayonet, the latest equipment in the British Infantry. General Ismay is at extreme left and General Sir Bernard Paget is at right.

office, all bearing the firmly penned initials 'W.S.C.' at their foot. Generals and planners were told not to argue but to get the thing done. Ministers were sharply told that their job was to produce the plans and results asked for, and not to present the difficulties and complications of their tasks. Not for him, the Head of the Government, the niggling details. For him, only the Big Order and a report, in due course 'on one sheet of paper', that it had been carried out by some subordinate, high or low. 'Action This Day' was his watchword.

Supermen Exist

Field Marshal Sir Alan Brooke's war-time diaries are full of criticisms of Churchill, whose policies often conflicted with his: the free-thinking orthodoxy against the highly experienced professional soldier. After the war Brooke wrote, 'I thank God I was given such an opportunity of working alongside such a man and of having my eyes opened to the fact that occasionally supermen exist on this earth.'

Churchill at the site of the El Alamein victory. The Casablanca Conference had taken place 14–24 January 1943. Winston Churchill gives a speech to men of the 8th Army at Tripoli, Libya, on 7 February 1943.

Above: Churchill and Montgomery at Tripoli. *Below:* Visiting British troops. Churchill wanted to meet the 11th Hussars, they had been the spearhead during the 1,600-mile advance of the 8th Army from El Alamein.

The Prime Minister wanted to see his Middle East Forces in action. Here, at an advanced outpost of the 8th Army, he is flanked by Generals Alexander (left) and Montgomery (right).

Code Names

The PM sent a firm memorandum to General Ismay on 2 August 1943 to the effect that he should approve code names before they were used. The choice of code names was fraught with psychological pitfalls — you could not use overconfident words, such as 'Victorious' in operations in which many people could be killed; neither could you use a gloomy or apocalyptic word — 'Woeful', 'Useless', 'Breakable', 'Catastrophe' would not inspire confidence in the men involved; and frivolity was not a good idea — words such as 'Bunnyrabbits', 'Titfer', 'Babybabble' would convey a lack of seriousness. Churchill went on to stipulate that ordinary everyday words should not be used for fear of confusion, and names of living people should be avoided — 'Operation Churchill' would be a bad idea. The names of ancient heroes, or mythological figures were acceptable — 'Boadicea', 'Beowulf', 'Zeus', for example; constellations or stars, such as 'Cassiopeia' or 'Arcturus'; even famous racehorses — 'Watling Street', for example, which won at Epsom the year before, but probably not 'Battleship', 1938 Grand National winner. (Race horses yes — but race meetings? ... This author fought in Epsom, almost in Goodwood and was wounded in Ascot!)

Churchill on board HMS *Renown*, returning from the Quebec Conference, with duffle-coated daughter Mary to his left hand. The conference, codenamed "Quadrant"), took place at the Citadelle and at the Château Frontenac, Quebec City, 17–24 August 1943. It was a highly secret military conference between Winston Churchill, Franklin D. Roosevelt, and William Lyon Mackenzie King. The allies agreed to begin discussions for the planning of the invasion of France, codenamed "Overlord". There were also discussions to increase the bombing offensive against Germany and continue the build-up of American forces in Britain prior to an invasion of France. In the Mediterranean they resolved to concentrate more force against Italy, an area Churchill had referred to in November 1942 as the 'soft underbelly of the Axis'.

Above: The Cairo Conference, codenamed "Sextant" was held 22–26 November 1943, at the residence of the American Ambassador, Alexander Kirk, near the Pyramids. The conference addressed the Allied position against Japan and made decisions about post-war Asia. Seated are Generalissimo Chiang Kai-shek, Franklin D. Roosevelt and Winston Churchill.

Below: Roosevelt and Stalin joke about Churchill's karacul hat at the Tehran Conference, 28 November 1943. The conference, a strategy meeting codenamed "Eureka", was held 28 November – 1 December 1943 at the Soviet Embassy in Tehran. The hat was a birthday gift from the British Press Unit.

The Sword of Stalingrad is a jewelled ceremonial long-sword specially forged and inscribed by command of George VI as a token of homage from the British people to the Soviet defenders of the city during the Battle of Stalingrad. Churchill presented it to Stalin at an afternoon ceremony during the Teheran Conference in the presence of President Roosevelt and an honour guard.

Stalin gives Churchill a birthday toast; Anthony Eden is standing to Churchill's right, looking toward the camera. Despite the bonhomie, Stalin was in the strongest position at Teheran and Yalta. He was well-informed about his allies. In Britain, a group of spies known later as 'the Cambridge Five' provided him with all the classified Foreign Office documents he needed. And from America, Alger Hiss, a Soviet spy working for the US State Department actually succeeded in becoming a member of the American delegation to the later conference at Yalta. Roosevelt believed he had a special personal relationship with Stalin – 'he hates the guts of all your top people,' he told Churchill. Meanwhile, Stalin baited Churchill. He teased and niggled him all the time. In one conversation, Stalin suggested that 50,000 German army officers should be shot. When the Americans appeared to agree, Churchill walked out in fury.

Above left: Churchill gave a birthday dinner party at the British Legation on 30 November 1943. He looks thoughtfully at the 69 candles on the cake donated by President Roosevelt and Marshal Stalin.

Above right: Winston Churchill recuperating, December 1943.

The Chinese Mandarin

For much of November and December 1943 and January 1944 Churchill was either ill or very ill. Part of this time he spent in Cairo, Tehran, Cairo again, Tunis, ancient Carthage and finally in Marrakesh to recuperate. His travelling doctor, Lord Moran, telegraphed for a pathologist (Pulvertaft), a heart consultant (Bedford) and two nurses to attend and look after the patient. On Christmas Day, dressed in his quilted dressing gown decorated with gold and blue dragons, Churchill entertained five Commanders-in-Chief and their staffs, son Randolph and daughter Mary to luncheon in the 'White House' in Carthage. The CIGS Alan Brooke thought the Prime Minister looked like a Chinese Mandarin.

Operation Shingle

This bold plan was to effect a joint American/British force landing at Anzio, thirty miles south of Rome, under General Mark Clark. The object was to threaten to cut off the German defenders of Rome and those impeding the Eighth Army advance from the south. On 22 January 1944, the British 1st Division landed north of Anzio and the 3rd US Division to the south. The

A Giles cartoon from The *Daily Express*, 30 December 1943.

German General Kesselring reacted quickly and within 48 hours had sealed off the bridgehead. Amazingly, 22,000 Allied vehicles had been landed and Churchill commented in a letter to the C-in-C Mediterranean, Admiral Sir John Cunningham, that they must have excellent chauffeurs. But it was not the success he had hoped for. Hitler gave orders that the bridgehead — or 'abscess' as he called it — be eliminated in three days. It was a near-run thing. After 125 days of battle, 40,000 out of the 110,000 Allied troops in the bridgehead were casualties. Churchill had hoped that the Allied forces were hurling a wild cat ashore instead of a beached whale on the shingle!

Hitler's Table Talk: 'Military Idiots'

'If Churchill says he leaves it to us, in our fear, to speculate where the second front will come, I reply "Churchill, you have never made me afraid." But you are right. We must speculate where the second front will come. Had I in front of me a serious opponent, I could figure out where the second front would come. But with these military idiots one never knows where they will attack ...' — which is presumably exactly what Churchill intended — doubt and more doubt.

Doubts about 'Overlord'

Ever since the calamity of Dunkirk in 1940 and the disaster at Dieppe in 1942, Churchill had been lukewarm and very cautious about a large-scale head-on invasion of Europe and the penetration of Hitler's Atlantic Wall. He feared that very heavy casualties might cripple the British Army. But he was under immense pressure to open the Second Front by Stalin and by President Roosevelt. When the Big Three (Churchill, Roosevelt and Stalin) met in Tehran in late November 1943, Stalin asked, 'Did the Prime Minister and the British Staffs really believe in Overlord?' (The operation was, incidentally, previously called 'Imperator', 'Bolero', 'Sledgehammer' and 'Round-up'.) Churchill still prevaricated, observing that if the conditions for the operation were favourable it would be their duty to launch every force they could muster across the Channel at the enemy. A month before D-Day, 6 June 1944, he wrote to the Dominion Prime Ministers to say that the United States were determined to invade north-west Europe, and that he had been unable to persuade them to go along with his preferred plan, which was to approach from the south and join up with Russian forces.

US troops disembarking at Omaha Beach, 6 June 1944.

The *Daily Mirror*, 2 May 1944.

Tank landing craft disembarking vehicles.

The Genius of Mulberry

The young Churchill's idea, developed in July 1917, was for a weatherproof harbour, like an atoll, made of flat-bottomed barges constructed of concrete, which when empty would be towed to their destination. On arrival, sea-cocks would open, and the barges, now filled with water, would sink, settle on the sea bottom, then be filled with sand by suction dredgers. Mulberry, in 1944, descended from Churchill's idea. Indeed, in 1942 Churchill directed Admiral Mountbatten that floating piers be designed to float up and down with the tide. The sad Dieppe raid proved conclusively that head-on attacks on defended enemy ports were doomed to failure. In August 1943 Churchill approved a major construction project involving a million tons of steel and concrete: 'Phoenix' concrete caissons, blockships ('Gooseberries'), floating pier units ('Whales'), Lilo and Bombard floating steel breakwaters. It was planned that 12,000 tons per day of supplies would be landed at each of the two Mulberry harbours, one in the British and the other in the American sectors of the D-Day beach landing areas. Arromanches, the British Mulberry site and the US Mulberry ten miles to the west were composed of 8,000 yards of blockships largely made up of eighty old merchant ships and four obsolete warships. Churchill confided, with some understandable pride, to Marshal Stalin on 7 June 1944 (D-Day+1) the very secret plan to build two artificial harbours on the estuary of the Seine. Mulberry was vital in the logistical battle to break the Atlantic Wall.

Breakwater of the concrete caissons of the Mulberry Harbour.

Hitler's Nightmare. *Le Petit Parisien*, 6 April 1944.

Success of Overlord

After the failure of Operation Jubilee — the Dieppe disaster — Adolf Hitler was convinced that it would be a very long time before the Allies made a large-scale attack on his Atlantic Wall. He knew it was inevitable but he hoped to subdue Russia on the Eastern Front and then repulse or beat the Allies in the west. The COSSAC planners — the Chiefs of Staff to the Supreme Commander Allied Forces — for Overlord and Neptune (the great naval attack) had produced a brilliant blueprint for Overlord. General Montgomery fine-tuned and strengthened the size of the attacking forces. The French Resistance and SOE sabotaged many French rail circuits. And there were at least five 'magic' ingredients: Ultra reading all the German defence signals; Mulberry harbours to bypass the immediate need for a port; Pluto to get oil piped swiftly across the Channel; Hobart's 'Funnies' or 'swimming tanks' (amphibious dual duplex Sherman tanks); General Patton's phantom US Army in southeast England 'threatening' the obvious Channel ports; the Allied air forces achieving total supremacy over the battlefields; and eventually, the astonishing bravery of the D-Day troops who landed on Sword, Juno, Gold, Utah and Omaha beaches and the airborne divisions floating in from the air. Churchill sent a message to Stalin on 7 June (D+1) that they had crossed the Channel with few losses — not the 10,000 they had feared — and hoped to have, by that night, some 250,000 men, armour and tanks on Normandy's beaches. Churchill visited the Normandy battleground on 12 June and on 22-23 July to confer with Eisenhower and Montgomery.

Operation Foxley

An SOE file released in 1998 gives details of Operation Foxley (these records are now held at the National Archives in Kew, London). Soon after D-Day, June 1944, Churchill approved a detailed plan to infiltrate Hitler's Alpine retreat in the Berghof, outside Berchtesgaden, and kill the Nazi Führer. An assassin was recruited but the SOE had doubts about the plot's feasibility. Regardless, Hitler soon retreated into his bunker in Berlin.

The Churchill Tank

A powerful British-made tank called the Churchill supported most infantry formations with its 6-pounder gun and machineguns. It was slow, reliable, ponderous and could take a great deal of punishment. (In July 1942, Churchill remarked to the Commons, 'It had many defects and teething troubles, and when these became apparent the tank was appropriately rechristened the "Churchill".') It had a ferocious cousin — the Churchill Crocodile, which towed a petrol bowser and hurled flames up to 100 yards ahead. It was ideal for tackling pillbox and fortified defences and was a singularly nasty and effective weapon.

A Churchill tank in Normandy, June 1944.

A Giles cartoon, The *Sunday Express*, 27 August 1944. *"If I am captured I would much prefer regular execution by beheading in the Tower of London to the farce of a noisy trial in Madison-square."* — Extract from Mussolini's Diaries, published in the North Italian Press. On 24 July 1943, Mussolini was defeated in the vote at the Grand Council of Fascism, and the day after the King had him arrested. On 12 September 1943, he was rescued from prison in Gran Sasso in a raid by German special forces on the direct orders of Adolf Hitler. Following his rescue, Mussolini headed the Fascist Republic in parts of Italy that were not occupied by the Allies. In late April 1945 he attempted to escape north, but was captured and executed near Lake Como by Italian partisans. His body was then taken to Milan where it was hung upside down at a petrol station.

Operation Anvil: Liberating the French Riviera

The Americans and General de Gaulle's French troops were far keener than Churchill on a joint attack — Operation Anvil — to liberate the South of France. Churchill feared that it would be at the expense of the main Operation Overlord. He was overruled, and on 14 August 1944, Churchill, aboard a British destroyer, observed the Allied landings on the Riviera, off St Tropez. As he watched, he saw, rising along the length of the lovely beaches, clouds of smoke from fires caused by shells. The troops landed with few losses. Three days later, in Naples, after de Gaulle had sent him an insolent letter refusing to meet, Churchill wrote of his concern that de Gaulle's France would be more antagonistic towards Britain than they had been since the two nations' quarrel over Egyptian Sudan in 1898.

The Third Front and Interlude in Italy

The Italian campaign, despite Mussolini's ignominious downfall, was long, and fought in appalling conditions on a narrow front that the German General Kesselring defended with great skill and tenacity. Twenty experienced Wehrmacht divisions defended the various lines — the Gustav, Gothic and Adolf Hitler. Field Marshal Alexander commanded a huge army of American, British, Canadian, New Zealand, South African, Indian and Brazilian forces. He called it the 'Third Front', possibly to show Stalin that the Allies were doing all they could to help keep the Russians fighting.

In August 1944 Churchill had an exciting interlude in Italy. He met Marshal Tito wearing a magnificent gold and blue uniform, drove with General Alexander around the terrifying Monte Cassino battlefield, addressed the Brazilian Brigade and inspected the New Zealand Division. He visited the US General Mark Clark at Leghorn and fired a brand-new nine-inch gun and, on the 27th, observed the battlefield as the Eighth Army launched an attack. He recalled that he heard more bullets there then than at any other time during that war.

Pacific Intentions. *Manchester Daily Dispatch*, 13 September 1944. The Second Quebec Conference, codenamed "Octagon" was held in Quebec City, 12 – 16 September 1944. Agreements were reached on Allied occupation zones in defeated Germany, the Morgenthau Plan to eliminate Germany's ability to wage war, continued US economic aid to the UK, and Royal Navy participation in the war against Japan.

Arnhem: 'The Bridge Too Far'

Field Marshal Bernard Montgomery had won all his battles by meticulous planning, and huge artillery and RAF bombing, and was generally regarded as a cautious commander who had never lost a battle (apart from the British Expeditionary Force in 1940). The plans for 'Market Garden' were daring and imaginative — completely out of character. The dropping of three airborne divisions (two American, one British) to seize vital targets; the linkup by British and Polish ground forces along one or two roads — a logistical nightmare — usually under fire from all sides; the casual dismissal of the photographic evidence that two German Panzer divisions were refitting in the Arnhem area — all these major risks were alien to the Montgomery of the desert and Normandy. Churchill put a brave face on the battle in his memoirs, remarking that, heavy as they were, these risks were almost vindicated. The eight-day battle in September 1944 came to be known as 'The Bridge Too Far'. Great heroism was shown, particularly by the three airborne divisions, but the plunge into the vitals of the Reich was firmly halted.

Operation Market Garden was the largest airborne operation in history. Over a three-day period 1,759 aircraft conveyed 34,600 men — 14,589 landed by glider and 20,011 by parachute.

Paratroopers
at Oosterbeek
near Arnhem, 18
September 1944.

Tube Alloys and the Manhattan Project

Since 1939 scientists had recognized that the release of energy by atomic
fission was a possibility, and in August that year Churchill talked frequently
with Professor Lindemann about nuclear energy. A paper on the subject was
sent to Kingsley Wood, Secretary of State for War, which was later code-
named 'Tube Alloys'. Secret research continued, mainly in the universities of
Oxford, Cambridge, Imperial College (London), Liverpool and Birmingham.
Coordination of work lay with the Ministry of Aircraft Production advised by
a committee of leading scientists under Sir George Thomson. In the summer of
1941 Thomson's committee reported that there was a reasonable chance that
an atomic bomb could be produced before the end of the war. The 'Prof' and Sir
John Anderson, Lord President of the Council, kept Churchill fully informed.
In October 1941 President Roosevelt was briefed by Churchill on the basis
of pooling all information, working together on equal terms and sharing the
results. For reasons of security (and perhaps cost) future developments (the
Manhattan Project) would be made in the USA. Imperial Chemical Industries
(ICI) in Britain released Mr W. A. Akers to take charge of 'The Directorate
of Tube Alloys'. Reports of German experiments with 'heavy water' reached
Churchill — hence a daring raid by SOE and the Norwegians which damaged
a vital German 'heavy water' plant, Norsk Hydro in Norway, and set back
enemy development. A number of key British scientists went to the USA to
work on the Manhattan Project (some of them rather too loyal to the USSR).
Goebbels's diary of 21 March 1942 noted, 'Research into the realm of atomic
destruction has now proceeded to a point where results may possibly be used

in the present war. It is essential that we should keep ahead of everybody'
On 21 March 1944 so much progress had been made that Sir John Anderson
suggested to Churchill that the War Cabinet and the Russians be kept informed.
Churchill replied to the first point, 'I do not agree. What can they do about it?'
And to the second: 'On no account.'

In 1947, two years after Hiroshima and Nagasaki, John Wilmot, Minister
of Supply, committed a ministerial committee of six to the manufacture of a
British atomic bomb. In 1951 Churchill heavily criticized Prime Minister Attlee
for the lack of success over five and a half years of atomic work!

The Fourth Moscow Conference, codenamed "Tolstoy" was held 9–19 October 1944,
but Roosevelt did not attend and was represented by US ambassador, Averell Harriman.
Issues discussed at the conference were the Soviet Union's entry in the war against
Japan, post-war division of the Balkans in the form of the 'Percentages agreement', and
the future of Poland.

Operation Tolstoy: Division of the Spoils

At the Moscow conference (Operation Tolstoy) starting 9 October 1944, Churchill, Eden, Alan Brooke and their entourage were lodged in dachas outside the city. Four days after arriving Churchill wrote to Clementine that all was going well and added that he had enjoyed his talks with Stalin, whom he was coming to like more and more. He also was party to what he called a 'naughty document' which spelt out spheres of interest in the Balkans. The horse trading — for that is what it was from Churchill's point of view — ended up: Romania — 90 per cent to Russia, 10 per cent to others; Greece — 90 per cent to Britain and the USA, 10 per cent to others; Yugoslavia and Hungary — 50 per cent to Britain and the USA, 50 per cent to Russia; Bulgaria — 75 per cent to Britain and the USA, 25 per cent to Russia. There was no mention of Poland. Stalin, when he heard the translation, took a blue pencil, made a large tick and passed the piece of paper back to Churchill. Stalin of course had not the slightest intention of adhering to this piece of paper.

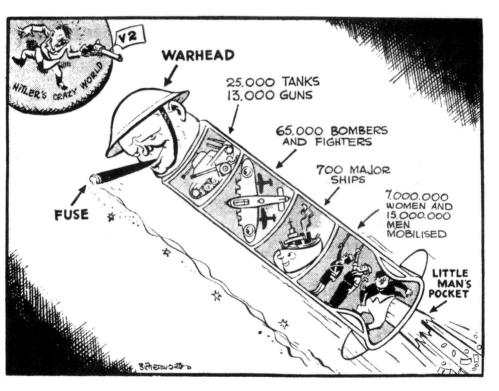

And we mean 'V'. Too! *Manchester Daily Despatch*, 29 November 1944. London and south-eastern England were menaced by V1 flying bombs and V2 rockets at this period.

General Charles de Gaulle making one of his BBC broadcasts to France.

Paris Again: Warning about de Gaulle

Churchill, Clementine and Subaltern Mary Churchill flew to Paris on 10 November 1944. The city had been liberated by General Leclerc's French 2nd Armoured Division (with very considerable help from General Patton's Third US Army). Appropriately, at 11 am on 11 November, General de Gaulle led a victory parade down the Champs-Élysées to the Arc de Triomphe where Churchill laid a wreath on the tomb of the Unknown Warrior. The splendid escort of the Gardes Républicaines in full uniform and the British Brigade of Guards detachment were leading the parade — both much admired by Churchill. He was none too happy about de Gaulle, however, writing to Anthony Eden: 'This menacing and hostile man [de Gaulle] will be a great danger to peace and to Britain in the future.'

The Greek Dilemma

In October 1944 Greece was on the brink of civil war between well-armed Communists and pro-Monarchist groups. A British force under General Scobie was sent to keep the peace, but in the first week of December violent fighting broke out on the streets of Athens. It became so serious that on Christmas Eve, Churchill and Anthony Eden flew to Athens where they met General Alexander and Harold Macmillan. On arrival Churchill was driven through the streets in an armoured car. A German-inspired plot to blow up the Hotel Grande Bretagne where the conference was taking place was foiled. Churchill insisted that the Greek Archbishop chair the tricky agenda and an uneasy peace was brokered. But, as he remarked in a letter to Clementine, the hatred between the Greek Communists and the Greek Monarchists was intense.

On Christmas Day, 1944, Winston Churchill and Anthony Eden conferred in Athens with representatives of the various conflicting Greek political parties. Above, Churchill and Eden are on the right of the Greek Regent, Archbishop Damaskmos, next to him is Harold Macmillan, the British Minister Resident for the Mediterranean.

The Battle of the Bulge — Hitler's 'Wacht am Rhein' in the Ardennes, began with Von Rundstedt's offensive on 16 December 1944 and petered out on 25 January 1945. This photograph of 28 January 1945 shows troops of US 82nd Airborne Division with improvised camouflage, dragging an ammunition sled near Herresbach, Belgium.

A Favour from Stalin

The appalling 'Battle of the Bulge' fought in mid-winter snows in the Ardennes caused immense casualties to the Americans and Germans and the British 'longstop' troops. Adolf Hitler called it 'Wacht am Rhein' ('The Watch on the Rhine') as part of a (superb) web of deception. The savage fighting continued into January 1945 and the experienced American General Patton wrote in his diary, 'This war can still be lost.' On 6 January Churchill sent messages to Marshal Stalin in Moscow seeking a major Russian offensive during January. Stalin, for a variety of reasons — one possibly even being because Churchill stressed that it was imperative — cooperated. But it was a close-run thing.

Brendan Bracken, Man of Mystery

During the election campaign of 1923-4, Brendan Bracken, a youngster of twenty-three, organized Winston Churchill's publicity campaign for the Westminster Abbey by-election. He drove round the West End in a coach and four with a trumpeter. Churchill, standing as the 'Independent and Anti-Socialist Candidate', failed to win. Bracken was a man of mystery; born in Ireland, he travelled and lived in Australia, was educated briefly at Sedbergh School and at one stage was rumoured to be Churchill's son. At Chartwell, Sunday was known as 'Brendan Day' when he descended like 'a fountain without pause ...' He entertained everyone with political information, gossip and anecdotes. A charming man, he became a close friend of Churchill's. He became a Conservative MP, Parliamentary Private Secretary, Minister of Information and eventually was made a Privy Councillor. He was also a journalist and a banker and never left Churchill's side as an adviser, but was regarded by many as a political lightweight. John Colville, Churchill's Personal Secretary, wrote in his diary in 1945: 'Tuesday, January 9 ... About midnight, while Lord Beaverbrook and Brendan [Bracken] were closeted in the PM's bedroom, having come no doubt on some nefarious intrigue...'

Independence

Churchill had his circle of intimates but Major-General Sir Ian Jacob, Assistant Secretary to the War Cabinet, noted, 'He had a remarkable independence of mind. No one ever had the Prime Minister in his pocket. Many who did not know him imagined that Lord Beaverbrook, or Brendan [Bracken], or the Prof had a great influence on him, or that one or the other could get him to do this or that. Nothing could have been less true.'

The Yalta Conference, codenamed "Argonaut", was held in the Livadia Palace near Yalta, 4–11 February 1945. By this time President Roosevelt was seriously ill and he died three months later, 12 April 1945.

The Yalta Conference: Operation Argonaut

The Black Sea resort town of Yalta was dubbed by Churchill 'The Riviera of Hades'. Travelling as Colonel 'Kent' with his daughter Sarah, they flew in his American C-S6 Skymaster to Malta, then transferred to HMS *Orion* and conferred with US General George C. Marshall and Admiral Ernest King, US Chief of Naval Operations. On their arrival at Sevastopol the huge entourage was berthed on the liner *Franconia*, the HQ for Argonaut. Stalin was ailing and President Roosevelt was to die ten weeks later, on 12 April 1945 Churchill stayed, heavily guarded, at the Vorontzov villa in Yalta, 5-11 February. The Soviet HQ was in the Yusupov Palace, from which Stalin carried out the control of their immense battlefronts. On the agenda was the treatment of Germany after the war. Should France have a zone of occupation in Germany? What about German reparations? Roosevelt told the meeting that they would only keep their occupation troops in Germany for two years. Who should be members of the Security Council of the World Organization agreed at the Dumbarton Oaks meeting? Poland was discussed at seven of the eight plenary meetings: where should the post-war borders be? And could 'Uncle Joe' be persuaded to declare war on Japan — quickly? President Roosevelt remarked that 'Poland has been a source of trouble for five hundred years.' Nevertheless, he urged totally free elections in Poland to decide its future. Stalin probably smiled sourly. Churchill then visited the battlefield of Balaclava where the Light Brigade had charged so gallantly and pointlessly in October 1854, and while there visited Lord Raglan's tomb, highly respected by the Russians. On the way home he had a rapturous welcome in Athens, and in Cairo met one Emperor (Haile Selassie), two Kings (Farouk and Ibn Saud) and one President (final meeting with FDR).

The Dresden Firestorm

Dresden was the capital of the old Kingdom of Saxony and famous as a cultural and aesthetic centre. It was in mid-February 1945 a major communications centre and near to the red Army's final offensive from Poland towards Berlin. The USAAF flew a daylight bombing attack and 786 RAF Lancasters flew across Europe and dropped 2,647 tons of bombs. Casualties caused by the resulting firestorm were enormous. In Churchill's minute he said 'It seems to me that the moment has come when the question of bombing German cities simply for the sake of increasing the terror, though under other pretexts, should be reviewed. Otherwise we shall come into control of an utterly ruined land.' He went on to criticise the policy of not concentrating upon military objectives, rather than mere acts of terror and mass destruction. By May 1945 all 60 of Germany's largest cities lay in ruins — the author's 11th Armoured Division passed through several of them.

On 13 February 1945 773 RAF Avro Lancasters bombed Dresden, followed over the next two days by 527 USAAF heavy bombers destroying the city and causing 25,000 fatalities.

The Rhine Crossing: Churchill under Fire Again

On 23 March 1945 Churchill flew by Dakota to Venlo in Holland and spent several days with Montgomery (now Field Marshal), watching the well-planned crossing of the river Rhine. This time the airborne divisions (6th British and 17th American) dropped quite close to the river. The two Scottish divisions, 15th and 51st, made successful crossings under the barrage of 2,000 guns. Churchill much enjoyed himself and had a picnic lunch with Montgomery on the banks of the river. He listened in as Montgomery's brave young battlefield 'inspectors' produced their individual reports — which provided valuable alternative or supporting viewpoints to those written up in official documents. Then he met General Eisenhower and went across the Rhine into enemy territory. They walked peacefully in the sunshine for some thirty minutes, until they reached the big iron-girder railway bridge at Wesel, when they came under fire, shells falling, first about a mile away, then nearing to a hundred yards, landing in the river, creating great jets of water.

General Dwight D. Eisenhower with Winston Churchill a few months earlier in France.

The Rhine Crossing: 'No more sand castles'

The American General William Simpson warned Churchill: 'Prime Minister, there are snipers in front of you: they are shelling both sides of the bridge and now they have started shelling the road behind you. I cannot accept responsibility for your being here and must ask you to come away.' Churchill agreed. As he put his arms around the girders of the bridge for a final time, Field Marshal Sir Alan Brooke recalled 'the look on Winston's face was just like that of a small boy called away from his sand castles on the beach by his nurse'.

General Slim and 'The Forgotten Army'

By March 1945, the Fourteenth Army under General William Slim had, after many ferocious battles at Imphal and Kohima, retaken Burma and killed or captured most of the Japanese invasion forces. Churchill later wrote that Slim and his army, through outstanding leadership, courage and resolute fighting, had succeeded in doing what had not seemed possible. King George VI commanded a special decoration, the 'Burma Star' to be struck on 9 May 1945. Nevertheless, many who fought under Slim regarded themselves as 'The Forgotten Army'.

The 'Forgotten Army' is an overlooked episode in history. With ferocious fighting against the Japanese, only two in ten of the soldiers who fought for the British in Burma were white, with around one hundred languages between them. They were led by General William Slim. Many soldiers came from all corners of the British Empire including 90,000 from Africa.

Operation Unthinkable

In April 1945 Churchill urged Roosevelt that Western troops should stay put, up to 150 miles into Soviet-designated areas of occupation. They would only be withdrawn when it was clear that Moscow was keeping its agreements on Eastern Europe. He also instructed 'Pug' Ismay, the Military Secretary to the war cabinet to draw up Operation Unthinkable, in which hundreds of thousands of British and American troops supported by 100,000 re-armed German troops would unleash a surprise attack upon their war-weary ally. Meanwhile the RAF would attack Soviet cities from bases in Northern Europe. But Churchill complained that nothing would convince the Americans of the Russian danger. Field Marshal Alan Brooke recorded that 'Churchill saw himself as the sole possessor of the [nuclear] bombs (due to be launched mid-July) and capable of dumping them where he wished, thus all-powerful and capable of dictating to Stalin.' However the Chiefs of staff argued that a more defensive type of study was needed in case the Soviets occupied France and the Low Countries. To the new American President Truman he wrote that Soviet Russia was now established in the heart of Europe. 'This is a fateful milestone for mankind.'

Wing or Drumstick? *Front National Paris*, February 1945. At the Yalta Conference Stalin proposed to carve up "the Nazi Bird" — Germany — between the Big Three.

Winston Churchill making a wartime speech, dressed in his siren suit — a one-piece garment with zip fastener which could be donned in a minute. He wore this at the White House during his 1943 North America visit, and the First Lady was so impressed she told her press conference she would have a similar garment made for FDR. Churchill designed it for himself so he would be comfortable during the long hours he spent in his wartime bunker. One version was made of pinstriped grey wool.

Speeches

'When the Prime Minister is going to make a speech he gives immense care and thought to every phrase, every word — to ensure that misinterpretation is impossible. When dictating a speech he will walk up and down the room deep in thought, murmuring and muttering to himself, while the uninitiated [Mary Thompson, his secretary, wrote] strains her ears to catch the almost inaudible words. When he is satisfied that he has found the right words, he will raise his voice and, at times, almost declaim his choice. He is such a great master of English that more than once I have found it difficult to keep my voice steady when asked to read back a particularly moving passage ... It gave me a feeling of immense pride and satisfaction to be an integral part of the "Top Secret" matters in war-time, to help to prepare speeches the whole world would hear.'

World's Press News, 26 April 1945. The end was in sight, the ring was closing in on Adolf Hitler in his Berlin Bunker. The Russians had entered the outskirts of Berlin and the Americans and British were advancing from the south and the west. Four days later Adolf Hitler shot himself.

Poisonous Politics

Churchill wrote to Clementine, 9 May 1945, a sober and thoughtful letter, enumerating the 'victories' — the numerous prisoners taken, the deaths of two dictators, the imminent surrenders to be made to the Allied forces — sadly recognizing that underlying the victory were poisonous and malevolent political rifts and hostilities.

The Real Churchill - 'fantastic'

In his book *Triumph in the West* Arthur Bryant wrote: 'What Alan Brook [CIGS] shows in his diary in the mingled exasperation and admiration of his day-to-day entries, is the real Churchill — the man who rallied a defeated nation in storm and disaster, passionate, impetuous, daring, indomitable, terrible in anger, pursuing every expedient — sometimes brilliant, sometimes, for he was prepared to try almost everything, *fantastic* — that could bring about victory.'

Victory in Europe

Harold Nicolson wrote to his son from Sissinghurst on 8 May 1945. Near the House of Commons he heard Winston Churchill's broadcast through loudspeakers: 'As Big Ben struck three, there was an extraordinary hush over the assembled multitude, and then came Winston's voice. He was short and effective, merely announcing that unconditional surrender had been signed, and naming the signatories. "The evil doers," he intoned, "now lie prostrate before us." The crowd gasped at this phrase. "Advance Britannia!" he shouted at the end and there followed the Last Post and "God Save the King" which we all sang very loud indeed. And then cheer upon cheer ... [At 3.23 in the House of Commons Chamber] a slight stir was observed behind the Speaker's Chair, and Winston, looking coy and cheerful, came in. The House rose as a man, and yelled and yelled and waved their Order Papers. He responded, not with a bow exactly, but with an odd shy jerk of the head and with a wide grin. Then he

8 May 1945. Winston Churchill and his cabinet appeared at the window of the Ministry of Health in Whitehall to a jubilant packed crowd. Six years of war were finally at an end in the West, but the East was still work in progress, and many more lives were yet to be lost. *Overleaf:* The view from the street.

started to read to us the statement that he had just made on the wireless. When he had finished reading, he put his manuscript aside and with wide gestures thanked and blessed the House for all its noble support of him throughout these years.'

'Dear Desert Rats'

Since the battle of Omdurman in 1898 Churchill had been fascinated by the North African desert which, from 1939 to 1943 was the only battle arena where his armies, with much support from the Dominions, took on the Italians and then Hitler's and General Rommel's forces. The Cherry Pickers (11th Hussars) led the British 7th Armoured Division, which in turn led the Allied armies across Egypt and Libya into Tunisia and final victory. Churchill followed very closely 'his' Desert Rats, their emblem being the tough, scrawny little jerboa rodent. In Berlin at the end of the war he told them that they were 'first to begin. The 11th Hussars were in action in the desert in 1940 and ever since you have kept marching steadily forward on the long road to victory. Through so many countries and changing scenes you have fought your way. It is not without emotion that I can express to you what I feel about the Desert Rats. Dear Desert Rats! May your glory ever shine! May your laurels never fade! May the memory of this glorious pilgrimage of war which you have made from Alamein via the Baltic to Berlin never die! It is a march unsurpassed through all the story of war ...'

Code Name Terminal: Babies Born Successfully

Churchill flew to Berlin from Potsdam on 15 July 1945 with Eden and Attlee. Polling day for the General Election had been ten days earlier and to allow the service votes to come in, three weeks extra were allowed. President Truman was the new American President, Roosevelt having died on 12 April. The British and Americans wanted the Russians to declare war on Japan — immediately. It was feared that it would take eighteen months and cost half a million Anglo-American casualties without Russian help. Stalin agreed but only declared war a few days before Japan surrendered! But during the conference, Henry Stimson, US Secretary for War, on 17 July handed Churchill a note: 'Babies satisfactorily born.' The atomic bomb tests in the Mexican desert were successful. There was now no need for Stalin's help in subduing Japan. An ultimatum to Japan was sent on the 26th, duly refused, and the bombings of Hiroshima and Nagasaki duly followed on 6 and 9 August.

The Nagasaki mushroom cloud. American and British scientists had worked on the 'Manhattan Project' since 1942. Two bombs were dropped from Boeing B-29 Superfortress *Enola Gay*, on Hiroshima 6 August 1945 and Nagasaki 9 August 1945. The shock of these events caused Emperor Hirohito to intervene and he ordered the Government to accept the terms the Allies had set down at Potsdam. After several days of negotiations and a failed coup d'état, Emperor Hirohito gave a recorded radio address to the Empire on 15 August 1945. In the radio address, called the Gyokuon-hōsō ("Jewel Voice Broadcast"), he announced the surrender of the Empire of Japan to the Allies.

Winston Churchill on the campaign trail.

'Finis'

One of the three Conservative election catastrophes took place in the twentieth century. The Tories were reduced to 210 seats and Labour won nearly 400. Churchill held Woodford (Epping had been split in two). On 26 July 1945 Churchill admitted defeat, went to the Palace that evening to see the King and resigned. The family spent a despondent last week at Chequers and Churchill signed the visitors' book and wrote 'Finis' underneath. He declined the Order of the Garter.

The Political Candidate

Winston Churchill was Member of Parliament for Woodford Division, Essex for twenty years (1945-1965). He fought in every General Election and in several by-elections after he stood for Oldham in a by-election in 1899 and was roundly defeated. But he succeeded in being elected in Oldham in 1900 and subsequently in NW Manchester, Dundee, West Leicester, the Abbey Division of Westminster and the Epping Division of Essex.

Churchill wrote every word of his many election addresses, one of the most vital factors in a campaign. He insisted on a complete door-to-door canvas by his loyal team and studied the reports every night. He would always meet all the workers chosen to staff his Central Committee Rooms, and was a firm believer in the use of display posters as widely as possible. At election meetings his devastating wit silenced hecklers and would-be wreckers; at the end of each meeting he liked to have the first verse of 'Land of Hope and Glory' sung before the National Anthem. Before polling day he toured his district in an open car from which he addressed *ad hoc* meetings, and which would be followed by a great cavalcade of press and radio reporters and photographers. He would single out small children for special attention. His wife Clementine helped him considerably, particularly at election time. Undoubtedly, he was not only a 'pro' in the House of Commons, but also in the hustings.

Tory Dream. *News Chronicle*, 30 May 1945.

They Haven't Changed a Bit! The *Daily Mail*, 4 June 1945. The first official train bringing evacuees home arrived in London.

Winston Churchill resigned as Prime Minister of the National Coalition Government on 23 May 1945, and formed a 'Caretaker Government' until Parliament dissolved on 15 June 1945. The General Election was held on 5 July 1945 and there was a landslide victory for Labour; they won 393 seats to the Conservatives' 197.

'In the Gloaming'

Field Marshal Alexander had offered Churchill the use of a villa on the shores of Lake Como after Potsdam and the General Election disaster. On 8 September Churchill, in maudlin mood, wrote to Clementine, recollecting an occasion years before when she had sung 'In the Gloaming' — a sentimental Victorian song — to him, rhapsodizing over the beauty of her singing, and the sweetness and pathos of the song. It had come into his mind, he told her, as he was driving Alexander's speedboat across the lake. He had painted nine pictures, advised by Charles Montag, Swiss-born and living in Paris, who arranged art exhibitions.

Future Full of Darkness and Menace: the Russian Iron Curtain

Churchill was now Leader of the Opposition to Clement Attlee's new Labour Government. On his way back from his holiday on Lake Como he was offered General Eisenhower's villa in Antibes, and, after two days in Monte Carlo (a rapturous welcome but no gambling), he painted a new Riviera series. He wrote to Clementine on 24 September from Villa Sous Le Vent, Antibes. He was nervous about the Russians, and viewed the future as sinister and threatening. He used, to describe Russia, a phrase that he had picked up some years before — 'iron curtain' — and which he was to make famous (and his own) less than a year later.

The 'Iron Curtain' Speech

In the presence of President Harry Truman, Churchill made a magnificent speech at (appropriately) Westminster College, Fulton, Missouri on 5 March 1946. He made it clear that 'I have no official mission or status of any kind ...

'The United States stands at this time at the pinnacle of world power. It is a solemn moment for American Democracy ... The awful ruin of Europe, with all its vanished glories, and of large parts of Asia glares us in the eyes.' He had high hopes of the United Nations Organization 'with the decisive addition of the United States ... is already at work ... [it is] not merely a cockpit in a Tower of Babel ... From Stettin in the Baltic to Trieste in the Adriatic, an iron curtain has descended across the Continent ...' The phrase 'iron curtain' rang round the world and crystallized the start of the 'Cold War'.

In 1946 Churchill visited the United States. Accompanied by President Truman, he arrived at Fulton. There, in an address on 5 March, entitled "The Sinews of Peace," he urged close unity between the United States and the British Commonwealth and Empire. This would involve collaboration between military advisers, similarity of weapons and instruction manuals, interchange of officers and joint use of bases. Eventually there might come the principle of common citizenship. The speech aroused widespread interest and, in the House of Commons, Mr Attlee stated that Mr. Churchill was speaking for himself only; the Government had no knowledge of the speech.

Beware the Bogy Man. The *Daily Mail*, 13 March 1946. The Soviet Union regard the Fulton speech as flagrantly anti-Russian.

The Pasha at Home

As the grandson of a duke, Churchill once said, 'My tastes are simple. I like only the best.' He lived the life of an aristocrat: great houses, regal surroundings, always servants and a valet at his beck and call. Clementine compared him to a pasha, clapping his hands for his servants to appear as he entered one of his houses. He was pampered. His hot bath was run for him, they dried him, they dressed him (one would put his socks on), they fed him and nurtured him with fine food, cigars and drink. He was a benevolent despot and made his secretarial staff work very hard (certainly during the Second World War).

Co-operation

Austen Chamberlain introduced Churchill to a Hungarian who lived in Paris called Imre Revesz (which later became Emery Reves). He ran an agency called 'Co-operation' which syndicated either first or second rights of articles or books to a wide, mainly European, market. In 1937 Churchill exchanged nineteen letters with him and although 'Co-operation' usually took 40 per cent of syndication fees, this still earned the author £2,000 per annum. No extra work was involved since only second rights for Churchill articles to foreign language markets were sold or syndicated. In 1946 Revesz visited Churchill in Miami and negotiated a deal for *The Second World War* whereby the non-English-language rights went to 'Co-operation' for a large sum. Reves made a considerable profit and purchased the beautiful La Pausa house near Roquebrune which Churchill used as a holiday home and where he spent eleven enjoyable (painting) visits. Reves did a similar deal with Churchill's *History of the English Speaking Peoples* in 1956–58.

'How it Melts': Chartwell Secured

Lord Camrose (William Berry), a newspaper group tycoon and good friend of Churchill, led, in November 1946, a syndicate which purchased Chartwell for £43,800 and presented it to the National Trust. Churchill and his family were then allowed to live there for fifty years at a modest rent of £350 per annum. In 1946–47 Churchill acquired the valley Chartwell Farm, Parkside Farm, Bardogs Farm and a market garden at Fleet Street — altogether he farmed 500 acres. His outgoings were always very considerable. 'How it melts,' he lamented as his assets dwindled — 'but not now'. He needed £12,000 a year to live on.

With grandchildren at Chartwell, November 1951. This photograph was taken on the same day as the group photograph on p. 231.

Literary Riches But All Rather Dull

Immediately after the war Churchill owned three extremely valuable literary properties — his future autobiography, his private archives and his Second World War memoirs. *The Daily Telegraph* paid £550,000 for his war memoirs to a new Trust, the Chartwell Literary Trust, of which Clementine was chairman, and Lindemann and Brendan Bracken co-trustees. *The New York Times* and *Life* magazine paid $1,150,000 for serial rights and Houghton Mifflin $1,250,000 for book rights in the USA. Further large sums came from Alexander Korda, London Film Productions, Henry Luce and Columbia Studios — altogether almost £200,000 for his other books. His bank balance stabilized at about £120,000. He formed a team to research the six volumes of *The Second World War* which appeared during 1948–54. Clementine took Volume III and others to task — it 'was all rather dull'.

Chartwell Regime

Churchill's bedroom had a controlled room temperature of 74° Fahrenheit (23° Celsius). A hearty English breakfast arrived each morning with his 8 o'clock call. He read all the day's papers in bed before starting work. Whilst he dressed he dictated to a secretary or wrote memoranda. After luncheon — delicious food chosen by Clementine accompanied by wine and brandy — he would walk in the gardens which he had created, to feed the golden orfe or waterfowl on the lake or work on his various wall-building activities. Two hundred bricks laid a day represented his usual output. Then followed his Cuban-style siesta which refuelled his energy for hours of further work — a considerable dinner — then either a cinema film or continued labours, often until 4 am.

'Butterflying All Day'

As a child Winston wrote to his mother, Lady Randolph Churchill, from Blenheim: 'I am never at a loss while I am in the country for I shall be occupied with butterflying all day'. He called butterflies 'flying fairies' and when Chartwell in the Kent Weald was purchased, he created a Butterfly Walk. Both Blenheim and Chartwell had Butterfly Houses. Inside shelves have cages of caterpillars on feed plants such as nettles, hawthorn and thistle. The chrysalids are kept in hanging anti-spider nets and the butterflies are released by finger 24 hours after they emerge. The planting at Chartwell is dictated by the butterflies' needs. In the summer and autumn there are buddleia, sedum, hebes, lavender and kitchen garden herbs. So Painted Ladies, Orange Tips, Red Admirals, Skippers and Tortoiseshells – all Churchill's 'flying fairies' – can be seen every year.

On Animals

In his biography of Churchill Piers Brendon wrote that 'he was very keen on animals. He had an anthropomorphic attitude to them. He had budgerigars, goldfish, cats, dogs and he loved pigs. You name it, he loved it. He treated them like human beings and talked to them... He was absolutely devoted to animals.' Toby, the budgie, was even allowed to peck his cigar — presumably not lit at the time — and occasionally went for rides in Winston's car.

Clementine's Pen Mightier than the Sword: ' I don't argue with Winston'

Clementine knew that when she expressed her deeply felt convictions verbally, particularly about political personalities, Churchill would (lovingly) demolish her contributions and views. So she took her time and wrote those views, sympathetically, shrewdly and occasionally trenchantly. To avoid a row or being ignored, if she had anything of importance to tell her husband, she would put it in writing.

Wot, stay in the same cage as that wild man, not me! The *Daily Worker*, 3 May 1949. The *Daily Worker* was the Communist Party newspaper and interestingly the word 'Fulton' is visible on one of the paintings in the cartoon.

'His Friendship was a Stronghold'

From 1906 the young Violet Asquith (later Bonham Carter), daughter of Herbert Asquith, was a close friend of Churchill's, and remained so until his death. In her biography of him (*Winston Churchill as I Knew Him*), she wrote: 'Those were red-letter nights for me. I forsook the [dance] floor, threw all engagements to the winds, cut dances right and left, sank deep into a sofa by his side and talked — or rather, listened to him talking ... he was impervious to his surroundings, blind and deaf to the gyrating couples, the band, the jostling, sparkling throng ... For him human beings fell, roughly, into three categories: the great figures whom he weighed, measured and assessed in a historical perspective and about whom his judgement rarely erred; the (so-called) average man and woman who often made no impact on his attention, let alone his mind; and lastly his friends — those who had found their way into his heart.

'His friendship was a stronghold against which the gates of Hell could not prevail. There was an absolute quality in his loyalty, known only to those safe within its walls. Their battle was his own.'

When Churchill became Prime Minister again at the end of 1951 he helped Lady Violet, a dedicated Liberal, to challenge the Labour constituency in Colne Valley by refraining from putting up a Conservative candidate. Moreover, he personally addressed a meeting in Huddersfield with her. It was not quite enough. 'The valley is still aglow with your presence,' she wrote to him.

The Sport of Kings

Horses in the army and polo ponies had been part of Churchill's life since he was a small schoolboy. After the Second World War, his son-in-law Christopher Soames encouraged him to enter the horse-racing world. His father, Lord Randolph, had owned horses and Churchill adopted his racing colours of pink and chocolate sleeves and cap. His trainer was Walter Nightingale, whose stables were at Epsom. A small stud farm was acquired at Newchapel Green, Lingfield, managed by Major Carey-Foster, a vet who was responsible, with Soames, for finding and breeding Churchill's horses. In 1952 he owned Pol Roger, Loving Cup, Non-stop, Gibraltar III and Prince Arthur. Irish horses he owned included Red Winter, Cyberine, Pigeon Vole, Pinnacle and Le Pretendant. However, Colonist II was the most successful, winning thirteen races, including, in April 1950, the 'Winston Churchill Stakes' at Hurst Park, and earning prize money worth £13,000. The grey French colt was popular with the public and was eventually sold to stud. Altogether, Churchill's horses won seventy races and he was elected a member of the Jockey Club and the Thoroughbred Breeders Association. Ownership gave him a lot of fun. His letters to Clementine were full of news about his stable of horses.

'Words Are the Only Things Which Last for Ever'

Churchill always wrote for the widest possible readership. Some of his favourite words in his books and articles were 'sultry', 'courage', 'solid', 'grim', 'vast', 'bleak', 'fearsome', 'immense', 'audacious' and 'formidable'. His eye for detail was amazing. He was meticulous with his publishers, pruning or polishing his text on the galley proofs, an expensive method of editing, but for him it was important that the final published product should be just so — for it would be read by millions and for many years into the future. Sir Isaiah Berlin described his style as 'Heroic, highly coloured, sometimes over-simple and even naïve but always genuine.' As Churchill once wrote: 'Words are the only things which last for ever.'

Authorship: 'We Shall Not Starve'

Churchill, once established as an author, was highly methodical, following a planned series of steps. Once a book contract with a publisher was signed, Churchill camps were set up, intelligence gathered, reports compiled. Many research assistants were employed, a number of whom became notable historians in their own right. They collected documents, appropriate references, bibliographies, and marked the key passages. They would check facts, prepare summaries, even pencil first drafts. He would farm out the work. For instance, Eddie Marsh composed 2,500-word outlines for Churchill's *The World's Greatest Stories Retold* at a modest £25 a draft. His master expanded the opus to 5,000 words and charged £330 for the finished article! 'We shall not starve,' he promised Clementine as his literary revenue poured in.

Paintings: a Follower of Cézanne

From 1915 Churchill painted for another forty years with advice from Lady Lavery, Sir John Lavery, Paul Maze, Sir William Orpen, Sir William Nicholson, James Sleator, Charles Montag, Walter Sickert and others. He painted wherever he went on his travels: Deauville, Lake Como, Dreux, Monte Carlo, Hendaye, Cannes, Cap Ferrat, Lugano, Maggiore, Genoa, Athens, Antibes,

Eze, Momizan, Marrakesh, the Pyramids, and above all, at Chartwell. In 1927 Sickert wrote him two 'teaching letters' on the technique of preparing canvases and how to make use of photographs as aides-memoires to plan paintings.

In 1948 Churchill was elected 'Honorary Academician Extraordinary'. Two years later Sir Gerald Kelly, President of the Royal Academy Committee picked out four paintings (out of seven) sent to them under the name David Winter. These were *Mont Sainte-Victoire, the Cassis Calanque*, a Carezza sketch and a snow scene (from his studio). Churchill described himself as a follower of Cézanne. In January 1958 a travelling exhibition of his paintings went to America, Australia and New Zealand. The next year his one-man show opened in the Diploma Gallery in the Royal Academy. Over 100,000 visitors were recorded. Some of his better-known paintings were *Winter Sunshine, Long River, Alpes Maritimes, Goldfish Pond at Chartwell, Blenheim Tapestries, Blue Sitting Room, Trent Park 1934, Cross on St Paul's Cathedral*, and *A Distant View of Venice*. In his lifetime Churchill produced hundreds of elegant, colourful oil paintings, some of them signed 'WSC'.

Churchill was forty before he discovered the enjoyment gained by painting. Over a period of forty-eight years he created more than 500 pictures and his art quickly became a passion. To him it was the greatest of hobbies, and escape from the hectic world of politics. This photograph appears to be in the south of France, probably late 1930s.

Winston's Aliases

At Harrow, Churchill wrote essays for the Harrovian school journal, exposing some apparent shortcomings in the school's administration, using the pseudonyms 'Junius Junior', 'De Profundis' or 'Truth'. With the 4th Hussars he rode in various Challenge Cups as Mr Spencer and in the Malakand Frontier Campaign his by-line was 'By a Young Officer'. During the war he was sometimes 'Former Naval Person' or on overseas, possibly dangerous, visits 'Mr Bullfinch', 'Air Commodore Frankland', 'Mr Green', 'Colonel Kent', 'Air Commodore Spencer' and 'Colonel Warden'. In later life, after being elected to the Royal Academy, Churchill was entitled to exhibit six of his paintings at the annual Summer Academy. He often used the pseudonyms 'Mr Winter' or 'Charles Maurin'.

Music Hall Varieties and Favourite Songs

Churchill enjoyed a good sing-song, his favourite songs being 'Run, Rabbit, Run', 'Me Old Cock Linnet' and 'Ta-ra-ra Boom-de-ay'. The Great War song 'Soldiers of the Queen' he sang with gusto. And happy tunes from *The King and I* and *The Wizard of Oz* would cheer him up. Noël Coward's catchy little 'Mad Dogs and Englishmen' and 'Don't Let's Be Beastly to the Germans' were particularly apt. Treasured possessions included gramophone records of *The Brigade of Guards Massed Bands*, *Forty Years On* (one of the Harrow School songs) and Gilbert and Sullivan's comic operas. One tune that saddened him was 'Keep Right On to the End of the Road' but his was a fairly cheerful collection in the main. One night he went to the old Empire Theatre, Leicester Square to see Fred and Adele Astaire in *Lady Be Good*.

The Pasha on the Move

On the move, Churchill was the centre of a Roman phalanx — an entourage of a dozen attendants — secretaries, personal servants, researchers, a doctor (Charles Wilson, later Lord Moran), a nurse, detectives or bodyguards (Inspector W. H. Thompson). And of course Clementine, or a daughter or Randolph, plus a crony or two (the Prof, Beaverbrook, Bracken or F. E. Smith). He always travelled first-class, drove in his deluxe Daimler, ate at the best restaurants, stayed at the most luxurious hotels in London or Paris or the Riviera, drank vintage champagne (usually Pol Roger), the choicest brandies and smoked the finest Cuban cigars. He was a welcome guest at palatial homes (where there were quite a few dukes), villas and yachts (belonging to friendly millionaires like Onassis). He enjoyed every minute of it and was totally unaware of everyday living. Clementine once commented, 'He knows nothing of the life of ordinary people.' During the General Strike, he tried the London Underground and became completely confused, got lost and had to be rescued. The 'pasha' on the move.

The Churchill Family Nicknames

Churchill was Pig, Pug or Amber Dog to his wife. She was Kat, Cat, Pussie, Pawser, Mrs Grimalkin (traditionally, the name for a witch's cat, or familiar), Clem-Pussy-Bird, and, rather disarmingly, Sweet Duck. Their infant offspring were the Kittens or Puppy Kittens or PK. Diana was Puppy Kitten, Sarah was the Mule or Bumble Bee, Randolph was Chumbolly, CB or the Rabbit, Mary was Maria and poor little Marigold, the Duckadilly. Brother Jack's family were the Jagoons, his wife Gwendoline was Goonie. Mary's husband, Christopher Soames, was the Chimp.

Churchill strongly criticized Soviet policy at the Conservative Party Conference at Llandudno on 10 October 1948. "Nothing stands between Europe today and complete subjugation to Communist tyranny but the atomic bomb in American possession," he said. If the United States consented to destroy their accumulated stocks of atomic bombs, he declared, they would be guilty of murdering human freedom and committing suicide themselves. Churchill was aware of the Russian Alsos — an operation which took place in early 1945 in Germany and Austria, with the objective of exploiting the German atomic related facilities, intellectual materials, resources, and personnel for the benefit of the Russian bomb project. They succeded and Russia tested its first bomb in 1949.

'He thinks like a Tory, and talks like a Radical, and that's so important nowadays.'
Oscar Wilde, *Lady Windermere's Fan*, Act II. *News Chronicle*, 10 March 1950. Herbert
Morrison and Clement Davies mistrust Churchill's Liberal-minded speeches.

Prime Minister Again

When Clement Attlee's Labour Government was beaten by the Conservatives
on 25 October 1951, Churchill became Prime Minister, and aged nearly
seventy took on a new lease of life. His radio broadcast on 8 November was
brilliant and he spoke to huge audiences in Liverpool, Newcastle, Plymouth,
Glasgow and of course, in Woodford. The Tories inched home in his
seventeenth election. He brought into his Cabinet his old friends Lord Ismay,
Field Marshal Alexander, Lord Woolton, Lord Leathers, Lord Cherwell, Lord
Salisbury, Harold Macmillan, his son-in-law Duncan Sandys and the ailing
crown prince Anthony Eden. Britain in the early 1950s had full employment
and was the second richest major country in the world. Churchill made four
official transatlantic visits, four by air and four in the old *Queen Mary* and
Queen Elizabeth.

The King, George VI, died in February 1952, and Queen Elizabeth II's
Coronation took place on 2 June 1953. Churchill had a stroke that month
and his doctor Lord Moran was doubtful whether he would live. But on 12
September, he and Clementine, on their forty-fifth wedding anniversary went
to Doncaster Races for the St Leger and thence (on the Royal train) to stay
with the Queen and Prince Philip at Balmoral.

'Death Came as a Friend'

On King George VI's death Churchill broadcast to the nation. 'During these last months the King walked with death as if death were a companion, an acquaintance whom he recognised and did not fear. In the end death came as a friend and after a happy day of sunshine and sport, after 'Good Night' to those who loved him best, he fell asleep as every man or woman who strives to fear God and nothing else, may hope to do.'

On Queen Elizabeth's Accession

'A fair and youthful figure, Princess, wife and mother is the heir to all our traditions and glories never greater than in her father's days, and to all our perplexities and dangers never greater in peacetime than now. She is also heir to all our united strength and loyalty. Let us hope and pray that the accession to our ancient Throne of Queen Elizabeth the Second may be the signal for such a brightening salvation of the human scene.'

The Queen and Prince Philip dine with the Churchills at 10 Downing Street.

Power – a Heady Drink

Guy Eden, one of Britain's leading correspondents for a quarter of a century, was a close acquaintance of Sir Winston's. As one-time chairman of the House of Commons Press Gallery, he wrote: 'Beyond any question, Churchill likes power. I am convinced that — like almost every man or woman that I know in our public life — he cares not at all for the spoils of office and least of all for the financial side. But power he certainly likes, with all the deference and the ceremony that go with it. And looking back over his crowded life, this is, after all, not surprising, for power is a heady drink.'

Winston's Lords

When Churchill's party acquired power in 1951 with 321 MPs against Clement Attlee's 295 he brought back many of his trusted friends — who were also lords. Ismay became Secretary of State for Commonwealth Relations. Field Marshal Lord Alexander, Governor-General of Canada since 1946, was persuaded to become Minister of Defence. Frederick James Leathers, another lord, arrived to oversee transport, fuel and power. Frederick James Woolton, famous during the Second World War for Woolton's Pies, became Minister for Food and Agriculture. Robert Cranborne (Lord Salisbury) was brought back to the Foreign Office. There were others including Lord Gavin Simonds as Lord Chancellor and Walter Monckton as Minister of Labour.

'Not So Bad'

Winston Churchill was awarded the Nobel Prize for Literature on 6 October 1953. He had hoped for the Peace Prize. He was in Washington at the time of the ceremony in Stockholm and Clementine went there to receive the award. 'It is all settled about the Nobel Prize. £12,100 free of tax. Not so bad!'

Swansong

On 3 November 1953, Churchill's speech in the House of Commons about the appalling power of nuclear warfare was praised by Henry 'Chips' Channon, MP for Southend West, as 'brilliant, full of cunning and charm, of wit and thrusts, he poured out his Macaulay-like phrases to a stilled and awed house. It was an Olympian spectacle. A supreme performance which we shall never see again from him or anyone else.'

A family group, November, 1951, on the Pink Terrace outside Mrs Churchill's sitting-room at Chartwell. Standing on the left, Mr and Mrs Duncan Sandys (Diana, the eldest daughter); their son Julian sits in front of them. On Winston Churchill's knee is Emma Soames, daughter of Mr and Mrs Christopher Soames (Mary Churchill); Emma's brother Nicholas is seated on the cushion. On the right of the hammock stands Randolph Churchill; his son Winston sits between Winston and Clementine Churchill and his daughter Arabella is on Clementine's left.

The Chartwell Library: the Napoleon Bust

Churchill kept his personal treasures in his library. A painting of Lord Randolph with fierce black moustache and wild eyes; Lord Randolph's mahogany writing table; a drawing of Jack Churchill; a watercolour of Leonard Jerome (his maternal grandfather), looking haughty; a bronze cast of Lady Randolph's delicate hand; a piece of shrapnel that almost killed him in the Great War; his own Chancellor of the Exchequer's budget black box; and a porcelain bust of Lord Nelson — and curiously, one of Napoleon.

The Suez Crisis

On 29 July 1956 President Nasser seized the Suez Canal. Churchill wrote to his wife that he thought the French — whom at the time he found co-operative — and British Governments should act together firmly and forcefully to reclaim the Canal. He feared that Anthony Eden, the Prime Minister, would wait for America — busy watching Soviet Russia — before doing anything, and that the States would once again come to their aid too late. Clementine shrewdly asked her husband why Israel had not been asked to the London Conference on Suez on 16 August.

On 29 October Israel attacked Egyptian positions on the Sinai Peninsula. On the 30th Britain and France issued an ultimatum — the two factions should cease fighting and withdraw from the Canal, which France and Britain could then occupy. Unsurprisingly, Egypt rejected this and on the 31st British bombers destroyed the Egyptian air force. UN resolutions calling for a ceasefire were ignored and British and French forces began to advance along the Canal. The Anglo-French invasion was to end dismally when, finally, the United Nations voted overwhelmingly against military action and Eden was forced to order a ceasefire on 6 November.

At the suggestion of Jock Colville (head of his Private Office), Churchill wrote to President Eisenhower on 22 November asking for his co-operation in resolving the Suez crisis. Ike answered that Eden had failed to inform him about the joint Anglo-French military operation. A week later Colville asked Churchill if he would have acted as Eden had done. Churchill answered that he would not have dared — but had he dared, he would not have stopped.

Sir Winston Churchill resigned due to ill health on 5 April 1955 and was succeeded by Sir Anthony Eden, a man who also was not in the best of health. Eden resigned in 1957 following the Suez crisis and was succeeded by Harold Macmillan.

Croix de la Libération

In view of their stormy relationship during the Second World War, it was surprising that on 6 December 1958, President de Gaulle invested Churchill in Paris with the highest award in the land to those who had served with the Free French or Resistance during 1939–45. There were only two Britons to receive this honour: King George VI and Churchill. Clementine accompanied Churchill to Paris to watch him receive this great honour.

Churchill College, Cambridge

Persuaded by his friends Jock Colville and the Prof, Churchill caused this college, named after him in 1958, to be founded. It was a scientific, engineering and technological foundation, with Churchill donating £25,000 from his Eightieth Birthday Presentation Fund. In his address he commented on the scientific advances made by the Soviet Russians — at the time well in advance even of American scientists. British science was well in the rear. He hoped that the new college might help redress the balance.

His Hand Kissed

Randolph Churchill introduced his father to Aristotle 'Ari' Onassis on 12 January 1956. Onassis ingratiated himself with Churchill, who was particularly taken with having his hand kissed, and the Churchills became regular guests. Churchill went, sometimes with Clementine, for eight cruises in the superb yacht *Christina*. Ari was an excellent host and put his penthouse suite in the Hôtel de Paris, Monte Carlo, at Churchill's disposal. Unfortunately, in June 1962, Churchill fell in his bedroom and broke his hip. An RAF Comet flew him back to England on the 29th, the day after the accident and he spent two months in the Middlesex Hospital.

'The Form'

Muriel Thomson nursed Winston Churchill in his final years. She logged her meticulous instructions for his care in 22 pages of her small ring-bound notebook which she called 'The Form'. Either at 28 Hyde Park Gate in Kensington, or at Chartwell, Kent, she organized him. In the morning: 'Check the policeman on duty. When he rings his bell tell the chef first and take the papers up. Draw the blind, put bed jacket ready on the table, bird cage over on a shelf, breakfast (two lots), orange juice to cool in the fridge.' Later in the day: 'Whisky and soda; specs; cards; bird [Toby, the budgerigar] to be brought into dining room near his chair; tweeds; hanky in top pocket; boiler suit; slippers.'

Once Nurse Thomson accompanied Sir Winston for a holiday in Nice. And Toby went too!

The Ninetieth Birthday Party

The twilight years for both Churchill and Clementine were often rather sad. Their health was a constant problem. She had to seek cures in various European spas and he spent much of his time on the French Riviera, either staying in friends' luxurious villas or on their yachts. On 30 November 1964, his ninetieth birthday was spent at 28 Hyde Park, London. Clementine sang 'Happy Birthday to You'; over 70,000 birthday cards were received. He waved from time to time to the crowds gathered outside and rested in bed, listening to Harrow School songs. The family dinner-party menu was consommé, Whitstable oysters, partridge, ice cream, fruit, cheese and biscuits, a birthday cake, appropriate wines and brandy. His last visit to the Houses of Parliament had been on 27 July and the next day a deputation with all the political party leaders visited him and in his dining room presented him with a magnificent Resolution thanking him for his services to Parliament, to the nation and to the world.

Winston Churchill at the window, acknowledging well-wishers, 30 November 1964. He died on 24 January 1965 in his ninety-first year. Clementine died on 12 December 1977 in her ninety-third year. Her ashes were laid in her husband's grave.

Operation 'Hope Not'

Preparations had been made beforehand — Operation 'Hope Not' — for Churchill's funeral. He was awarded a State Funeral. The last great commoner to have this honour was the Duke of Wellington in 1852. For three days and three nights 321,000 people in bitter cold midwinter weather passed the catafalque in Westminster Hall, to pay their last respects to the great commoner. On Saturday 30 January 1965 the state funeral cortège left for St Paul's Cathedral. Big Ben chimed ten o'clock and was silent for the rest of the day. In St James's Park the first of ninety guns began their salute — one for each year of his life. A Union Jack covered his coffin. On top was a black cushion with the insignia of the Order of the Garter. Clementine led the procession in the Queen's town coach and Randolph followed the gun-carriage on foot. The three services took part — a Royal Naval escort and Guards and RAF bands marched in slow time to Handel's *Death March*.

In St Paul's a congregation of 3,500 included the Queen, five other monarchs, five heads of state and sixteen prime ministers. Eisenhower, General de Gaulle and Marshal Koniev were present. One hundred and eleven countries were represented. Twelve pallbearers carried the coffin through the nave to the catafalque, including Eden, Macmillan, Mountbatten, Attlee and Robert Menzies. Churchill's favourite hymns were played: 'Mine Eyes Have Seen the Glory of the Coming of the Lord', 'Fight the Good Fight with All Thy Might' and 'Oh God, Our Help in Ages Past'. Menzies' address from the cathedral crypt was broadcast to the world. 'In 1940 ... one man with soaring imagination, with fire burning in him, won a crucial victory ... for the very spirit of human freedom.'

After the service the coffin was taken to the Tower of London pier, piped aboard the *Havengore* (a Port of London Authority launch) and a small flotilla of launches carried the family upstream to the sound of 'Rule Britannia' and a 19-gun salute from the HAC guns at the Tower. Sixteen Lightning jet fighters swooped overhead as his coffin was conveyed up the Thames to Waterloo station from where the Battle of Britain steam locomotive *Winston Churchill* took him to Long Harborough. He was buried in Bladon churchyard next to his brother Jack.

Churchill's Uniforms

During the popinjay years 1895 to 1900, Churchill kept his tailor busy and purchased uniforms (paid for rather slowly) for the equivalent today of £30,000. *Inter alia* they included those of the 4th Hussars, Punjab Infantry, 21st Lancers and Lancashire Hussars; during the Great War he added the Grenadier Guards, Royal Scots Fusiliers, Elder Brother of Trinity House and much later an RAF Air Commodore! His Second-World-War 'zootsuit' was probably inexpensive.

Churchilliana – A Paradise

Churchill memorabilia is a collector's paradise, with interest always strong from America. In the last decade auction houses on both sides of the Atlantic have seen a doubling of value of Churchilliana. Some examples follow:

In 1998 one of his side arms sold for £17,000 and in 2002 one of his revolvers fetched £32,000. A complete set of books written by Churchill will fetch around £3,000. On eBay a first edition of *The Selected Essays of Sir Winston Churchill* dated from 1976 attracted 16 bids and went for £746. Some insignificant letters — signed of course — are always in demand and can fetch up to £3,000. A pair of his monogrammed blue velvet slippers reached £6,325 a few years ago, and a first edition of *Brodrick's Army and For Free Trade* published by Winston Churchill in 1899 went for £50,000. His paintings increase in value: his 'Mimizan, Landes', a view of the Duke of Westminster's house, was sold by Christies in 1998 for £150,000. And the great man's bits and pieces and ephemera will continue to be more and more valuable.

Societies

During the course of his career Churchill was Honorary Bencher of Gray's Inn, Chancellor of Bristol University, Honorary Academician Extraordinary of the Royal Academy, Honorary Fellow of the Royal College of Physicians, Honorary Fellow of the Royal College of Surgeons, Fellow of the Royal Aeronautical Society, Fellow of the Society of Engineers, Fellow of the Royal Society of Literature, Fellow of the Royal Institute of British Architecture, Fellow of the Royal Geographical Society, Fellow of the Institute of Journalists, Fellow of the Zoological Society, Honorary Member of Lloyds, Elder Brother of Trinity House and of course, Honorary Colonel of several Army Regiments, and an Honorary Air Commodore.

Churchill's Orders and Decorations

Companion of Honour (1923)
The Order of Merit (1946)
Knight Companion of the Most Noble Order of the Garter (1944)

The India Medal (1898) with clasp Punjab Frontier 1897-8

The Queen's Sudan Medal 1896-8 (1899)

The Queen's South Africa Medal 1899-1902 (1901) with clasps as follows: Diamond Hill, Johannesburg, Relief of Ladysmith, Orange Free State, Tugela Heights, Cape Colony

The George V Coronation Medal (1911)

The 1914-15 Star (1919)

The British War Medal 1914-18 (1919)

The Victory Medal (1920)

The Territorial Decoration (1924)

The George V Silver Jubilee Medal (1935)

The George VI Coronation Medal (1937)

The 1939-45 Star (1945)

The Africa Star (1945)

The Italy Star (1945)

The France and Germany Star (1945)

The Defence Medal (1945)

The War Medal 1939-45 (1946)

The Elizabeth II Coronation Medal (1953)

The Cross of the Order of Military Merit, Spain (1895)

The Cuban Campaign Medal 1895-8, Spain (1899)

The Khedive's Sudan Medal, with clasp Khartoum, Egypt (1899)

The Distinguished Service Medal (Army), United States (1919)

The Order of Leopold with Palm (Grand Cordon), Belgium (1945)

War Cross (with Palm), Belgium (1945)

Military Medal, Luxembourg (1945)

The Order of the Lion of the Netherlands (Knight Grand Cross), Netherlands (1946)

The Order of the Oaken Crown (Grand Cross), Luxembourg (1946)

Military Medal, France (1947)

War Cross (with Palm), France (1947)

The Royal Norwegian Order of St Olaf (Grand Cross with Chain), Norway (1948)

The Order of the Elephant, Denmark (1950)

The Order of Liberation, France (1958)

The Order of the Star of Nepal (First Class), Nepal (1961)

The High Order of Sayyid Mohammed bin Ali el Senoussi (Grand Sash), Libya (1962)

Bibliography

All quotations from Sir Winston Churchill are copyright © The Estate of Winston Churchill. For permission to quote from the literary works of Sir Winston Churchill application must be made to Curtis Brown, Haymarket House, 28-29 Haymarket, London SW1Y 4SP.

ASQUITH, H. H., *Letters of the Earl of Oxford and Asquith to a Friend* (Geoffrey Bles, 1934)

BACON, R., *The Life of Lord Fisher of Kilverstone* (Hodder & Stoughton, 1924)

BLOOD, B., *Four Score Years and Ten* (G. Bell, 1933)

BONHAM CARTER, V., *Winston Churchill As I Knew Him* (Eyre & Spottiswoode, 1965)

BRYANT, A., *The Turn of the Tide* (Collins, 1958)

CHARMLEY, J., *Churchill: End of Glory — A Political Biography* (Hodder & Stoughton, 1993)

CHURCHILL, R., *Winston S. Churchill* (Heinemann, 1967)

CHURCHILL, W. S.,
  — *My Early Life* (Macmillan, 1944)
  — *Thoughts and Adventures* (Odhams Press, 1947)
  — *Second World War*
    Vol. 1 — *The Gathering Storm* (Cassell, 1948)
    Vol. 2 — *Their Finest Hour* (Cassell, 1949)
    Vol. 3 — *The Grand Alliance* (Cassell, 1950)
    Vol. 4 — *The Hinge of Fate* (Cassell, 1950)
    Vol. 5 — *Closing the Ring* (Cassell, 1952)
    Vol. 6 — *Triumph and Tragedy* (Cassell, 1954)
  — *The World Crisis:1911-1918* (Free Press, 2005)

CHURCHILL, WINSTON S., ed., *Never Give In!: The Best of Winston Churchill's Speeches* (Pimlico, 2004)

COLVILLE, J., *Fringes of Power: Downing Street Diaries 1939-1955* (Hodder & Stoughton, 1985)

EADE, C., ed., *Churchill by his Contemporaries* (Hutchinson, 1955)

EDEN, F., *Portrait of Churchill* (Hutchinson, 1946)

GILBERT, M., *Churchill: A Photographic Portrait* (Wm Heinemann, 1974)
— *Churchill: A Life* (Pimlico, 2000)

HART, L., *History of the Second World War* (Cassell, 1970)

HOUGH, R., *Winston and Clementine: The Triumph of the Churchills* (Bantam, 1990)

HMSO Hansard (Commons and Lords)

JENKINS, R., *Churchill: A Biography* (Pan, 2002)

JONES, R. V., *Most Secret War* (Hutchinson, 1978)

KEEGAN, J., *Churchill's Generals* (Hutchinson, 1991)

LEWIN, R., *Churchill as Warlord* (Stein and Day, 1978)

MACKENZIE, N. and MACKENZIE, J. eds., *The Diary of Beatrice Webb* (Virago, 1986)

LORD MORAN, *Winston Churchill: The Struggle for Survival 1940-65* (Constable, 1960)

MOOREHEAD, A., *African Trilogy: The North African Campaign 1940-43* (Hamish Hamilton, 1944)

NICHOLSON, N. ed., *Harold Nicolson: Diaries and Letters 1930-1939* (Collins, 1967)

PATERSON, M., *Winston Churchill: His Military Life 1895-1945* (David & Charles, 1967)

PELLING, H., *Winston Churchill* (Macmillan, 1974)

ROSE, N., *Churchill: An Unruly Life* (Simon & Schuster, 1994)

SOAMES, M., ed. *Speaking for Themselves: The Personal Letters of Winston and Clementine Churchill* (Doubleday, 1998)
— *Clementine Churchill* (Doubleday, 2003)
— *Winston Churchill: His Life as a Painter* (Collins, 1990)

STAFFORD, D., *Churchill and Secret Service* (Abacus, 2000)

THOMPSON, M., *Churchill: His Life and Times* (Odhams Press, 1954)

THOMPSON, R. W., *Generalissimo Churchill* (Hodder & Stoughton, 1974)

TREVOR-ROPER, H., ed., *Hitler's Table Talk* (Weidenfeld & Nicolson, 1953)

WILMOT, C., *The Struggle for Europe* (Fontana, 1952)

WILSON, T., *Churchill and the Prof* (Cassell, 1995)